THE CHARM OF THE ANTIQUE

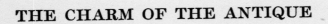

The Charm of
the
Antique

THE CHARM
OF THE ANTIQUE

BY

ROBERT AND ELIZABETH
SHACKLETON

ILLUSTRATED

THE PENN PUBLISHING COMPANY
PHILADELPHIA
1921

CONTENTS

ILLUSTRATIONS

ILLUSTRATIONS

ILLUSTRATIONS

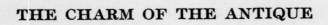

THE CHARM OF THE ANTIQUE

THE CHARM OF THE ANTIQUE

CHAPTER I

THE CHARM OF ACQUISITION

THE charm that pervades the antique, the allurement that comes with time, the fascination that accompanies the serene mellowing of age, are infinitely increased by possession. It is delightful to look upon a treasure of the past, tinged as it is with the tender grace of a day that is dead; but it is infinitely more delightful to make the treasure one's own. And the more that one gathers and loves, the more does there come a deeper enjoyment, a finer satisfaction, a fuller joy. The quest of the antique leads pleasurably on from one delightful triumph of acquisition to another.

Yet for worth-while collecting there must be a worth-while foundation. There must be a standard of taste and distinction. It must be fully appreciated that, contradictory though it may at first thought seem, the basic charm of the antique is not its age. There must

1

be something more than age; the passage of years cannot give delight unless there would be somewhat of delight even without the years. The antique must, in short, always and antecedently, possess the quality of beauty. But if a thing is beautiful, the hand of time gradually touches it with delectable fascination.

And beauty must not be taken in a narrow sense, for it properly holds within itself proportion, dignity, propriety, grace. Not only may a painting be beautiful, not only may statuary be beautiful, but a chair may be beautiful, a table may be beautiful, there may be beauty in a chest of pine.

If age alone were sufficient to constitute charm, the furniture disdainfully termed Victorian would now enjoy the beginning of a collecting vogue; for early Victorian furniture is old, and mid-Victorian and late-Victorian will soon be similarly old; yet these styles can never attract true collectors, for they are based on bad taste and the absence of distinction and beauty.

From the first, the true collector must absolutely realise that he must gather only the things that were always good, and that the thing that is undesirable can only achieve with age an added undesirability. "Is not every part about you blasted with antiquity?" demanded the Lord Chief Justice of Falstaff, with more than an implication that age had only made him worse.

There is always the agreeable reflection that collecting is not merely a matter of money, although it is true that some of the rarest and most beautiful treasures are only for the rich. For, rightly gathered together, with the charm of fitness and distinction and beauty added to the charm of time, one's treasures may be costly or may be the reverse; they may be priceless tapestries, lordly vessels of silver and gold, furniture superb with ornament and inlay, or they may be the chair rightly modelled, the table without ornament but of perfect lines, the chest of drawers that was not beyond the man of moderate means. It is line and proportion and colour and shape that are the essential factors.

Every one will remember Irving's alluring description of the home of Katrina Van Tassel on the Hudson, with its claw-footed chairs, its dark mahogany tables shining like mirrors, its glistening andirons, its rows of resplendent pewter, its corner cupboard with its treasures of silver and china. One loves the description, and knows that he would love the things themselves; first of all, because of the obvious fact of their beauty, and following that, because there would be added the subtle zest, the otherwise incommunicable charm, of age. Who would not love to find Katrina's treasures real, and to make delightful acquisition of them for his own!

No matter how much one's affectionate liking for an antique treasure deepens and strengthens with length of possession, there is never anything quite like the thrill that comes with the very moment of acquisition, that moment of ecstasy when the collector first holds, and holds as his own, something that he has longed for. The acquisition may be the unexpected good fortune of a happy moment, or it may be a triumph following the hope and desire of years; but no matter how it comes, it comes as one of the most delightful of sensations, a sensation that cannot in the least be understood by one who has never begun to collect. And not only are there manifold ways of attaining antique treasures, each with its thrill of felicity, of achievement, of keen delight in taking a treasure into personal ownership; but there may at the same time be, in multifarious forms, the pleasures that come from some special history of the prize secured, some reminiscent interest or delightful association.

Our latest acquisition—it was but of last week, for the collector never ceases from collecting; there is always the one thing more—was an exquisite little cup that, in its acquiring, gave peculiar charm. It is of Lowestoft—that is, what is universally called Lowestoft, although it was made at thousand-chimneyed King-te-Tching, and not at the English village to which it reached out for a name: Lowestoft, in the late eighteenth century, being a tiny fishing village with a little porcelain factory, and how the name became attached to a special kind of Chinese porcelain is a mystery that no one can solve and in regard to which only the most improbable conjectures can be made. The cup is of pearly tint, and on its side is a delicate, flowered medal-

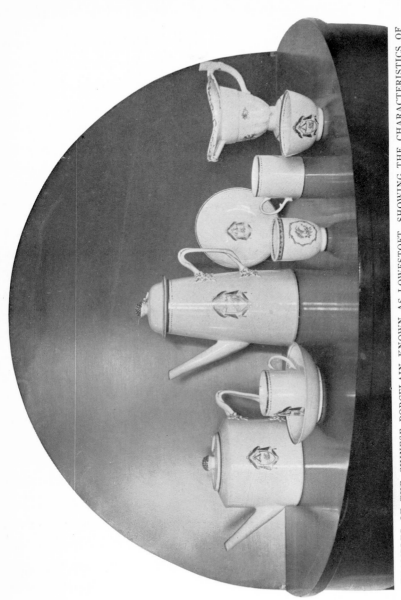

EXAMPLES OF THE CHINESE PORCELAIN KNOWN AS LOWESTOFT, SHOWING THE CHARACTERISTICS OF THE WARE; THE CUP DESCRIBED IN THE TEXT IS IN THE CENTER.

OLD BRASS FENDER FROM MARYLAND, SET IN FRONT OF AN OLD FIRE-
PLACE, WITH OLD BRASS ANDIRONS FROM OHIO, BRASS KETTLE AND
TRIVET AND BRASS-HANDLED TONGS.

lion encircled by a narrow band of lacquer-red and gold. Around its outside edge is an exquisite border, and around the inside edge is a border of equal daintiness, the work of the borders and medallions being marvellously small, and of infinite detail.

Far back, not far from 1790, a little girl was walking on a Philadelphia street with Nellie Custis, when a stately step sounded behind them. It was the step of George Washington. He slowed his pace as he came up with the two friends, and, taking a hand of each in one of his own, walked on with them. The little girl was almost overcome by the splendour of her experience, for, child though she was, she knew the immense awe in which Washington was held by the people of his time. It was an experience as brief as it was splendid; but to her it seems to have been the supreme happening of her life. She died, a spinster, an aged lady, and to the last loved to tell of that brief walk. And always, with naïve unconsciousness, she expressed the awe that she had felt by showing in her narrative that she had not dared to raise her eyes—for she could only tell, as to what he looked like, that he wore kneebreeches, dark stockings, and buckled shoes.

And this fine cup has come down to us from the hand that held the hand of Washington. It is the last piece of a set, older than our Constitution, that the girl's mother owned. And the daughter inherited the pieces, and one by one they broke or vanished, until, when she too was old, and there was but this cup left, she gave it to a little girl, who is now just seventy-one, and is the old lady who passed it on to us.

And this simple little old-time experience, clinging to a little cup, brings vividly a vision of the long-past time—the streets, the homes, the people, the great Washington himself; it makes history seem as of the present day, it summons up remembrance of things past, it illustrates the potential charm that may lie in the acquisition of the antique.

Acquisition may be made in quite a variety of ways, of which buying at an auction is one of the most fascinating, for in this are the tingle of contest, the thrill of triumph, and the satisfaction of feeling that your own judgment in paying a price is backed by the judgment of your rivals who come within a tiny distance of the figure you reach. It is a game of finesse, of strategy, of boldness.

At an auction in the country there may often be found some long-desired treasure, and the prices will not average very high. There can be no greater contrast with such a sale than the auctioned breaking-up of famous collections in the great cities, when men battle with each other in mounting thousands for the possession of rare and priceless things. Every collector gets some of his things at auction, either expensively or, more commonly, the reverse. And always there is the sense of triumph and delight.

Some four or five years ago, we went to a country auction sale near Bernardsville, New Jersey, passing on the way through Morristown, of Revolutionary fame, and Basking Ridge, where Revolutionary soldiers warmed themselves in the sun because they had no blankets. One comes to realise that the quest of things of the past may take one to many a place of interest.

The auction was in an ancient stone house of chocolate brown, a house with ancient box-bushes in the garden, a house rich in alluring promise to the lover of the old. And it was a disappointment to find that the family had decided to reserve all the precious pieces from the sale, leaving scarcely anything of interest. However, the pleasure of the drive would repay us for the time, and meanwhile we did not lightly give up hope.

The auction was in progress when we arrived, and in a little while there was put up a chair completely upholstered in padded and wadded calico, beruffled and befrilled. It was apparently an ordinary bedroom chair—and yet there was something about it that aroused the sixth sense that every collector should possess. Really, it seemed as if the size, the proportions, the vaguely indicated shape, could mean only one thing. There was only a moment to spare, and it was possible in that moment to reach out and feel beneath the calico —and there were a little round foot and a slender ankle, and the surmise was correct.

There was no eager bidding for the humble-seeming

chair. The auctioneer perfunctorily set it forward. An old lady offered a quarter. And that was all. The chair did not appeal to the country-folk, nor to the swarm of collectors who, like ourselves, had been drawn by the fascination of the old house and the expected old furniture. A nod to the auctioneer and for thirty-five cents the chair became ours—an armchair, an exquisite example of what is known as "Sheraton fancy"; golden brown, with touches and pattern of dull gold leaf—a real beauty, scorned in the dress of old calico.

We have a room in which the chairs are all Chippendales: one with arms, two of that very early design which really just preceded Chippendale, and two, the most honoured, of Colonial association.

One waited for us—or we waited for it!—for six years, before the moment came when we could call it our own. We discovered it in a house, built about 1725, which had been one of the finest Colonial mansions near Philadelphia, and which we visited on account of its architecture and design. But the house was in the sere, the yellow leaf, here and there fallen plaster marked fallen fortunes, and it had long ago come into the possession of a farmer whose son, himself become a very old man, now occupied it, or rather, occupied part of it, the rest standing empty and forlorn. And there we discovered the chair, a Chippendale of early and fine design, with bandy legs and web feet, and shell surmounting a jar-shaped splat; a chair of proportion and dignity, and almost surely the work of an eighteenth century Philadelphia maker, as it almost identically matches some chairs that were made in that city before the Revolution and were part of the furnishings of the Presidential Mansion when Philadelphia was the national capital.

Considerable old furniture, including five other chairs precisely like this, had passed with the old house to the long-ago farmer-buyer, but everything had been gradually disposed of, or worn out, till only this single chair remained. And instead of regretting what we missed of the past, we were happy in our discovery of this solitary survivor, for it is such delightful happenings that make the collector always confident that at the very next moment he will come upon some fascinating find.

But that chair the present owner would not sell. "I am going to give it to my son," he said. He was pleased, however, with our sincere admiration of the old house, and added: "But if I ever do sell the chair, it shall be to you."

We did not urge differently. To secure a piece by inducing an owner to sell against his will, when he wishes to hold it for an excellent and legitimate reason, would destroy the fine feeling that should accompany every acquisition.

So time went by, yet we never forgot that Chippendale. Once, three years afterward, we passed that way and called, but the chair was still destined for descent, and again we did not urge any disposal different.   Then another three years, and the farmer, greeting us, said: "I'm sorry I didn't let you have the chair, for the children have been playing with it, and one of them fell over with it and it's so badly broken you wouldn't care for it now.   I was going to burn it, but thought you might come along."

The chair was in an unused and cluttered room. And it was indeed a sad-looking wreck, for the entire top bar of its back was off.   However, the bar had been kept; all but an upper corner in front of the dowel-pin —a chip of the Chippendale—and on examination the case seemed far from hopeless.

And there was good fortune to come, for a brief search in the clutter actually unearthed the missing chip —a piece with a curve, that it would have been difficult to replace with exactitude.   The chair was at once bought, and has been so heedfully repaired that it is as strong as ever, and there is no apparent sign of the fortuitous break without which the treasure would never have become ours.

Another of the chairs is even finer and of even better proportions and workmanship, and the distinctive splat is of admirable open design.   It apparently came from England, and not unlikely from the hand of Chippendale himself, instead of from one of his host of followers, for it was part of the furnishings of a house of wealth and taste, such as in the early days was often out-

SIX CHIPPENDALE CHAIRS, SHOWING VARIED DESIGNS. THE CHAIR
IN THE LOWER LEFT HAND CORNER WAS OWNED BY ANTHONY
WAYNE; THE ONE ABOVE IT WAS OBTAINED AT AN OLD COLONIAL
MANSION.

THE HEPPELWHITE SIDEBOARD, WITH TYPICAL HANDLES OF THE
PERIOD; IT HAS A CONCAVE-CENTER, AND THE TWO APPARENT
DRAWERS AT THE LEFT ARE A DEEP WINE-DRAWER.

fitted from across the sea. The chair was, in fact, one of the belongings of General Anthony Wayne, and it came to us personally from one of the most respected citizens of eastern Pennsylvania, who had himself had it for thirty-five years.

This makes it what is known as a pedigreed piece, and adds greatly to its value, not alone in sentiment, but in very real and practical worth. Indeed, in this chair are represented the three phases of value, from a collector's standpoint: first, intrinsic beauty of form and workmanship; second, the charm of age; third, the fine additional charm that comes from definite history and from having been owned and used by a famous person of the past.

None of the other four Chippendales is quite the equal of these in distinction; but the fact that two of them were gathered at different points only a year ago, and for reasonable cost, in spite of the sometimes expressed belief that no more old Chippendales are to be had from original sources, shows what chances still await the collector who will search and wait and be ready to seize upon an opportunity.

A sideboard was acquired in a way that was all its own. We had waited years to find just the right one at a not prohibitive price, and our ideal was a Heppelwhite. But desirable sideboards suddenly seemed to grow elusive, evasive, coy. One chance was found, but was let go, on account of the temporary inconvenience of it, until it was too late; which was very unwise, for the collector should never miss a chance to secure what he really wants. It was a long time before a chance came again, for old sideboards are not easy to find.

We heard of an artist, reputed a good deal of a recluse, who owned two sideboards that were the fame of his neighbourhood, though few had seen them; and there was a vague suggestion that he looked upon one as a needless extra. We were not acquainted with him, and it was understood that he did not care to show his furniture to strangers. But fortunately, one of us met him one day in the office of a mutual acquaintance in New York, and the conversation turning—or being turned! —to furniture, sideboards were spoken of, and he made a rather grudging drawing of the one that, as he expressed it, he really had no use for. But his grudgingness seemed only his way of expressing pride.

He was not asked if he would sell; that would have been fatal to our chances and, indeed, a collector needs never to ask such a question direct, as it would be not only rude, but needlessly rude, there being various more politic ways of obtaining the desired information.

The drawing was of only one leg and one handle; but with the dimensions that he was able to give, it was quite sufficient to show that he possessed an unusual Heppelwhite sideboard, with original brasses. But he quite omitted to mention such points of excellence as that the front was recessed on a concave curve, that the mahogany top was unusually good, and that the big wine-drawer did not offer a bare expanse, but was fronted to look like two separate drawers.

He was perfectly frank in saying that the sideboard needed polishing and needed, also, a considerable amount of repair; and for fifty dollars, a very reasonable price for such a treasure, he sold it. It cost two dollars for freight and handling; it took precisely twenty-five dollars to put it in condition; and thus for seventy-seven dollars was acquired a fine and rare piece, rich in simplicity and dignity, a piece of vastly more value and distinction, even to one who is not a lover of the antique, than any modern sideboard that could be purchased for anything like that amount. It is what is technically known as a collector's piece, because it is not only completely authentic, but is at the same time of rarity and value, and an excellent example of style.

Visiting in an old Maryland town, we heard of a house in which was amassed much that was rare and old, which the mistress of the house might be willing to dispose of, as she was going to move away; the only cloud on the collecting horizon being, so it developed, that although the stuff was old, or at least sufficiently worn to look old, it was not rare, and it was not treasure. It was of the period of horsehair nonentities, but the dear old lady was so proud of it that it would have been heartless, and likely enough useless, to attempt to unde-

ceive her. From room to room we went on, as she affectionately pointed out her valueless things.

But in one room was a bit of real interest; a fine old
brass fender, and we hailed its discovery with joy. But
at once she was troubled. She would be glad to sell it,
but—it was very embarrassing indeed, she declared!—
she remembered that she had half promised to sell it to
a local fishman. She was so very, very sorry; but she
had given her word to the man of shad and oysters!

But inquiry developed that he had not promised to
buy the fender, although she had promised him the
chance, and in that lay the saving grace of the situation.

At once one of us set out in search of him; he was
not at his stall in the market; but fortunately he was
soon come upon beside his cart in the town. (It was
the second time that we had heard of a local fishman as
a gatherer of antiques; we long ago discovered that the
local undertaker often uses his opportunities to acquire
such things for re-sale; but this idea of the peripatetic
fishman being a speculative collector was rather surprising, and somehow seemed to have within it something amusing as well.)

"Do you wish to buy that fender?" The question
was put to him with a pleasant bluntness.

Yes, he certainly did. Whereupon it at once resolved
itself into a case of which of us was willing to pay the
larger sum for it, and as he did not care for it very

much from that point of view he promptly yielded his option for a dollar!

The dear old lady was immensely relieved by the adjustment of the difficulty; and the fender, capable, efficient, and fine-looking, became ours.

It stands in its new home, in the quiet dignity of old brass, in front of an ancient fireplace, with old brass andirons and brass trivet and brass kettle behind it, and old-time chairs on either side. And when the lights are lit and the fire sparkles on the hearth, myriad shining reflections glimmer and gleam and glow in the old-time brasses, as if glimmering, gleaming, and glowing to light pleasurable paths for the collector.

CHAPTER II

PLACED prominently in the Museum of Fine Arts in Boston, there is a notable painting by Copley, representing those two South Carolina aristocrats, the Izards. Mrs. Izard, slender of body, slim of face, formal, precise, distinguished, sits in front of heavy damask, in a heavy gilded armchair, beside a heavy gilded table topped with porphyry. Ralph Izard sits in another gilded chair at the other side of the gilded table. He, too, is slender of body and slim of face; he, too, is formal, prim, precise; and in well-tailored coat, in knee breeches, in silk stockings, he, too, is altogether distinguished.

The picture is interesting in itself, and becomes even more interesting when it is remembered that through the devotion of Izard to his country, he, wealthy man though he was, became so straitened that he was unable to pay the desired one thousand dollars to Copley for it, and died without possessing it.

But there is something odd about the picture. Were not its history so well known, any lover of old furniture might even suspect it to be one of the many paintings of doubtful pedigree. For where was such a table made? Where could Copley find such chairs? A painting of about the time of the Revolution, by an American, of two Americans, would be expected to show furniture such as stood in American houses of the period; furniture of American make, or such as would come from England, France, or Holland. That the Izard painting shows furniture that somewhat resembles Louis Quinze is all that can be said, but any one familiar with French workmanship sees at once that it was not made in France.

Yet the explanation in this case is as unexpected as it is simple; and the lover of old furniture finds his hesitant misgivings completely justified and at the same time completely removed; he finds that the usual late eighteenth-century style is not shown, because the portrait was made in Rome, where the painter and the Izards chanced at the same time to be, and the furniture is therefore Italian!

There is, indeed, a very delightful charm that comes from a knowledge of styles and periods in furniture, for one's pleasure is thereby broadened in so many ways; and not only does pleasure come from the knowledge, but often there is a very practical satisfaction as well, especially when one is not only looking at antiques but buying.

Nor is it needful to have a really exhaustive knowledge—from A to Izard, so to speak! A general outline is readily acquired, and beyond that it is difficult for even the expert or the student to go, for there is inherent in the subject a certain charming vagueness which leaves many of the border-lines indeterminate. One may know a Sheraton sideboard, a mid-eighteenth-century chest of drawers, an Empire of the fine first form; and then may hesitate as to whether a Windsor is a century or a century and three-quarters old, or wonder, as to a table, if it is of English or American make, and then merely date it as of somewhere in the eighteenth century. One may learn that the bonnet-top, the broken-arch, was first made in the reign of Queen Anne, that the twisted rope came in with the nineteenth century, that Chippendale flourished before Heppelwhite— and then cannot say with positiveness just when Chippendale sank and Heppelwhite arose.

But always, in spite of the vagueness, in spite of the merging of period into period, in spite of the persistence of some styles and the subjection of others, there is much of certainty possible. Alike when you own a piece or merely see it, your pleasure in the sight or the possession is vastly increased by knowing for yourself what it is you see or own and when and where it was made. The lover of the old should walk by sight, not faith; and even in those cases that demand somewhat of faith, it should be an understanding faith. With the gaining of a knowledge of periods and styles, there comes to collecting a new and intelligent savour, a finer charm.

And for the American of to-day, the important thing is to learn, first, all that he can about things that Americans can nowadays find, leaving the study of things older than the eighteenth century for quiet days at Cluny and Knole.

First of all, one somehow thinks of chairs; and most widespread in use of all old chairs are the Windsors. Whether or not the old tale is true that George the Second discovered such a chair in a cottage near Windsor and at once had some made for his own use, it is at least true that the Windsor is fitted for the home of either the rich or the poor. It is not, indeed, a chair of expensiveness; it is not for rooms of formality and elegance. It is a chair for the porch—Washington had thirty on his splendid stone-slab terrace at Mount Vernon; it is also a chair for indoor comfort even though not for the finest rooms—Washington had one in his bedroom; it is a chair for a library—Jefferson so liked the type that he sat in one to write the Declaration of Independence. It ought really to be called the Democratic chair, so wide has been the range of its ownership, use and usefulness; and that it won the practical approval of George of England and George of America only adds to its right to such a title.

Seldom are two Windsors precisely alike; yet always and unmistakably a Windsor is recognized. There is a curving back, of slender spokes of hickory or some wood similarly bendable; perhaps there are arms, and perhaps, although rarely, the arms are of mahogany, though all the rest of the chair is of ash and hickory; and perhaps at the broadened end of each arm there are grooves for the comfortable holding of the fingers; the seat is always solid and of one piece, probably of ash, and is heedfully hand-shaped; the legs are lathe-turned and set firmly into bored holes in the seat. Such is the Windsor, a shape always graceful, a chair competent, reliable, strong. And when a visitor tips back, laughing, in your Windsor, you don't have that sinking feeling—for he won't break it!

The vogue of the Windsor was, broadly speaking, from half a century before the Revolution to half a century after; and for that hundred years it remained a chair of the people, for the people, used by the people, regardless of the waxing and waning of evanescent styles.

Seven Windsors of our own will serve to illustrate not only some of the different kinds, but also, by the methods and places of their acquisition, will illustrate the varied opportunities that are constantly offering themselves to the collector who is watchful to see and ready to obtain.

The one on the left of the picture is from Province-town, that place on whose site the Pilgrims first set foot, before proceeding farther to find and found Plymouth, on its supposititious stern and rockbound coast—though about the only rock in the neighbourhood was

AN EXTENSION-BACK, COMB-BACK WINDSOR.

SEVEN WINDSOR CHAIRS, OF VARIED TYPES AND HISTORIES.

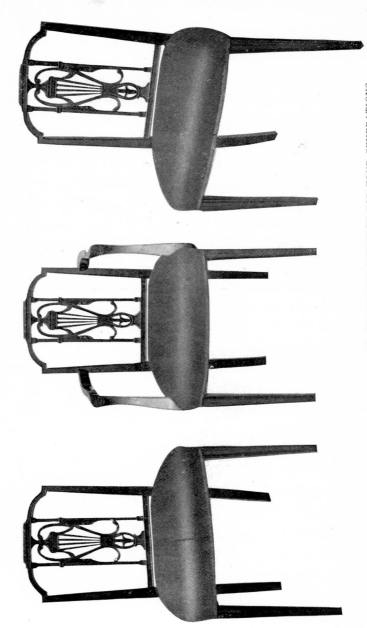

THREE ADMIRABLE SHERATONS, OF UNIMPEACHABLE PEDIGREE FOR FOUR GENERATIONS.

Plymouth Rock itself. At Provincetown we came to know an old and interesting captain, one of the many retired captains of the ancient seafaring town; but this captain being unique among captains, for since quitting the sea he had turned his attention to products of that element, and dealt in ambergris (name oddly full of mysterious fascination!) and porpoise oil, which oil he secured by boiling porpoise heads upon the beach, at which times it was olfactorily wisest to approach him from the windward side! In his attic was a collection of sword-fish blades and shark's teeth, Portuguese bottles, and the multifarious flotsam and jetsam of years that had led to even the remotest quarters of the globe. And there was one single article of Colonial kind—a Windsor chair; or, rather, just a legless back and seat!

"That! I used to think I'd make legs for it, but now I never shall;—and if you care at all for it just take it along."

So we took it along, for assuredly any kind of Windsor chair from Provincetown was worth while; and as to the deficiency of legs—well, one of us happened to notice, not long afterward in a little carpenter shop in a town of the early-settled Western Reserve, of Ohio, a set of legs, of Windsor type, without any back! "Just drifted in from an old house. Just take it along." So we took it along; thus learning anew how opportunely opportunity often comes—though not often does it actually give legs to the legless.

As to the next chair on the left—one of us, passing an old-time lyceum building, which had stood closed and unused for many years, noticed that it was open, with carpenters at work, the entire floor having fallen into the cellar. And there, half buried in the debris at the bottom, was a Windsor chair! It was pointed out to the contractor, who glanced down at it in puzzled scrutiny and said: "That chair? Probably smashed! But if you care for it you're welcome"; whereupon it became merely a matter of clambering down among fallen beams and flooring and as gently as possible getting at the ancient piece; not without some danger from further falling beams. And the chair was extricated without breakage, nor had it been broken in its fall with the floor!

The two chairs on either side of the one in the centre are different, it will be noticed, from the others, in having perforated splats down the middle of the back. That they also have what is called extension backs, is a point they share in common with some Windsors of America, like the one at the extreme right, but the splat is a feature, so far as we know, only of Windsors made in England. You see chairs of this type in many an old English home. Each of these chairs has unusual underbracing, which turns back in a sweeping curve.

The one at the left of the centre is of yew, and is very heavy, and was found, only last year, in that unpromising English city, from a collector's standpoint, Manchester, and cost only fourteen shillings in addition to the slight sum for getting it to the steamer at Liverpool.

Almost its twin, in appearance, is the one at the right of the centre, but it is made of lighter wood than yew; hickory, the usual wood for Windsors on our own side of the Atlantic, being only an American wood. This second chair came to us ancestrally, from the possession of a great-grandmother. Both of these were made in Yorkshire or its neighbourhood, as they are a type that we have seen there more commonly than elsewhere in Great Britain.

The chair in the middle is of 1790, and was made by a certain I. Henzey. Not infrequently, Windsor chair makers stamped or burned their names upon the bottom. This particular chair belonged to an old man of Williston Township, some thirty miles from Philadelphia, who, dying about 1865, gave it to a friend of ours, from whom we obtained it. And these details are given, to indicate what additional pleasure may come from precise—if veritable!—knowledge of the history of a piece.

This chair, a particularly graceful specimen, is three feet two inches in height and the top of its back measures two feet and five inches on the curve—this curve reaching back to a distance of six inches from a straight line. The top bar has just the desirable shapings, and is tipped slightly forward, giving it a comfortable touch that only an old-time hand worker would dare attempt by such means; and the ends are carved into dainty little ears, and the spindles are adjusted with heedful art, and the bracing crossbar, down below, has the desired "egg" in the centre, and in all it is an admirable example, slim and light but very strong. It is a tribute to the slenderness and charm of such Windsors that these backs are often called "fiddle-string."

The chair next to the end, on the right, is of the kind colloquially known as "balloon-back," and was obtained in the Mennonite region. It had been so well cared for as to have a tiny iron brace put in to prevent a crack from spreading; and its canny owner, "Pennsylvania Dutch," was well satisfied—and this was only three years ago—to have his offer of the chair for seventy-five cents accepted.

The chair at the right is unusually comfortable and is sturdy and strong as the day it was made, although that day was at least a hundred years ago. It was found in a busy modern town in which there were certainly some hundreds of people who would have liked to possess it. It was bought from underneath the local liveryman; one principle of collecting being that there are certain people who are glad to sell anything they have.

The cost was precisely a dollar and a half; and this would show, even to one unable to judge of the merits of the piece by itself, that it is an original old chair, and not something made to sell as an imitation, for chairs of this general kind, that are frankly reproductions, can only be made to sell for about four dollars each.

The other Windsor chair, photographed in two views, is a great armchair, whose extension back is itself a "comb-back"; a name whose origin is obvious, for the extension does sit up like an old lady's high comb; and it is an admirable chair, in size and dignity.

Not only the Windsor, but most other early American styles, came here from England. There was an early impress from Holland, which affected little outside of New York State; long afterward, the Napoleonic style known as Empire won great American popularity; but the great French styles, named after successional sovereigns, made little or no impress here— the Louis Quatorze, rich, dignified, and splendid; the Louis Quinze, with all the richness but without so much of dignified restraint; the Louis Seize, full of charm and delicacy. But during the prevalence of these great styles on the French side of the Channel, great styles arose in England that were promptly followed and adopted by ourselves, in importations and in the work of our own craftsmen.

The best-known English names are the great ones of Chippendale, Heppelwhite, and Sheraton; these three, but the greatest of these is Chippendale.

Thomas Chippendale made the years from about 1740 to 1780 the Chippendale period. He would not practise inlaying or veneering, although these arts were well known to him.   His furniture had to be beautiful and it had to be strong; and it had not only to be strong but to look strong.   He made fine shapes, in admirable proportions, with splendid craftsmanship.   He is especially noted for his chairs, a distinctive mark of which is the splat down the middle of the back, from the usually bow-shaped top to the seat.   His chairs are of generous size, appropriate for the voluminous costumes of that time; there is seldom a Chippendale chair of stinted narrowness.

The legs may be straight or cabriole, may be footed with claw and ball, may have the web foot or the spade foot, or may go straight down with no foot at all.

Whenever a Chippendale chair is referred to, without qualification, all collectors take it to mean the splat-back type; but there is also a "ladder-back Chippendale," a term which admirably describes the design; and the Chinese Chippendale, for Chippendale for a time followed after Chinese fretwork patterns and even lacquer—an aberration deplored by all who really love and appreciate him.

Although Chippendale made much furniture, it is not to be understood that a piece must have been made by him personally to be deemed a Chippendale.   He had a great many imitators and followers; in fact, he published a book of plans and directions on purpose to be imitated.   It was the same with Heppelwhite and

Sheraton, each of whom gave his name to a certain school or style, and each of whom set forth his ideas in a book for other cabinet-makers. So far as this single point is concerned, a Chippendale, a Heppelwhite, a Sheraton piece, need not have been made by one of the three personally, any more than a Louis Seize or a Louis Quatorze bit of furniture needed to be made by the king personally. In each case the name is the name of a style.

Furthermore, the styles named after the three Englishmen, although differentiated essentially upon differences in treatment and design, do not always represent literally what the three separately made or always stood for, but by the tacit agreement of decades of furniture lovers they have come to be class names, type names, *genre* names. If it could be shown that Heppelwhite personally made a chair in what is called Sheraton style, it would none the less be a Sheraton chair; if it could be shown that Sheraton made swell-front chests of drawers like those to which the name of Heppelwhite has been given, they would still be Heppelwhite fronts. Such use of the names has been adopted through the need for fairly definite nomenclature.

Pretty nearly any really fine piece of furniture, sturdy, dignified, beautiful, and without inlay or veneer, if made in the Chippendale period may fairly be called a Chippendale piece. It may be added that there are no Chippendale sideboards, in the present-day meaning of the word, as in his time side-tables served all sideboard needs.

The vogue of Heppelwhite was from about 1775 to 1795, lapping that of Chippendale on one end and Sheraton on the other. The typical Heppelwhite chairs have backs that are oval, heart-shaped, shield-shaped, or something similar. The style of Heppel-white is always full of grace and lightness and charm. He favoured inlay, and freely used it in bell-flower designs and dropping garlands and lines of contrasting colour. He loved the rich effects of whole areas of veneer. He used satinwood and many pale-coloured woods, as well as mahogany. He knew the use of paint for fine effects. There are beautiful Heppelwhite chests of drawers with swell-fronts, and there are long, graceful sideboards, and delicate and graceful side-tables with top that opens and leg that turns.

The typical Heppelwhite leg is slender and square-sided, tapering toward the bottom, and not fluted. The Heppelwhite foot—using the word for something shorter than a leg—has often a splay curve outward.

Sheraton was strong from 1790 to 1800; after that his style depreciated and his influence waned. But in his period of strength he and his followers made fine and beautiful furniture. In the general shape of tables and chests of drawers he much resembled Heppelwhite, but his name is not associated with the splay foot, nor did he make nearly such great use of inlay.

A CHARACTERISTIC HEPPELWHITE CHAIR, WITH SHIELD-BACK; AND
TWO EMPIRE CHAIRS, SHOWING THE INSPIRATION OF THE ROMAN
CURULE CHAIR.

A TYPICAL AND EXQUISITE WORK-TABLE OF HEPPELWHITE DESIGN.

AN EMPIRE TABLE OF THE PERIOD ABOUT 1825, WHEN THE STYLE WAS TENDING TOWARD DETERIORATION.

The typical mark of Sheraton is the fluting, or reeding, of the legs of his sideboards and tables, and of columns on the corners of his desks and chests of drawers. The legs are generally round, but are sometimes square-sided. The typical fluting is not common on his chair legs, his chairs being known by their backs, which are square or rectangular and end in a cross-rail a little above the seat.

That Sheraton could not quite appreciate the work of his close rival, Heppelwhite, is not at all surprising, but it is curious to find him referring rather patronisingly to that of Chippendale, as work that did, indeed, possess merit but was now wholly antiquated!

The Empire style began in France about the year 1800, and arose from the tremendous effect upon the popular imagination of Napoleon's campaigning in the East, and his own desire to have styles in furniture, as in everything else, that should reflect his own achievements. The winged claw, the griffin, the sphinx, came in, and also the twisted rope and a revival of the classical acanthus; through the revival of classicism there came, too, chairs inspired by the curule chairs of ancient Rome. The Empire style was, indeed, a compound of Egypt and Rome, and in a brief time began to deteriorate toward the ugly, the over-carved, the grotesque.

Our friendship with France, and our admiration of France—after the wave of horror that swept over us from the excesses of the early days of the French Revolution—were such as to make us ready to follow new French styles. We had not, indeed, followed the style of Louis Sixteenth, much though we loved France, because it was a very expensive style, and we were poor and were fighting for national life; but by the time of the Empire we were feeling the glow of coming strength and of coming prosperity, and eagerly followed the new designs of the great French nation, our friends; especially as they were no more difficult to follow than those coming from the English, whom we had already been fighting and were likely, as all knew, to be fighting again. And it is worth while noting that while Empire style in furniture was so cordially adopted, Empire style in woman's dress was also cordially welcomed, American women thus early learning to look to Paris for their fashions: the lead in this being taken by that woman of charming personality, affectionately known to generation after generation as Dolly Madison.

America, though adopting the Empire style in furniture with enthusiasm, adopted it at the same time with restraint, and made much Empire that was really beautiful, aided by the coming in at that time of great quantities of rich San Domingo mahogany. But even here the style before many years began to degenerate, and Empire pieces, of which there are still many obtainable, should be chosen with hesitant care. The sofa of which a picture is shown can be traced back definitely, as to ownership, to 1830, and was made about 1810 or 1812.

"This mahogany sofa," so reads the memorandum from
the old Pennsylvania lawyer, once the burgess of his
town, from whom we obtained it, "was in Judge Isaac
Darlington's parlour, in West Chester, in 1830. After
his death, it passed into the possession of Daniel Nields
of West Chester, from whom I bought it about thirty
years ago." It has been in our possession for a dozen
years. And it adds to the interest and value of any
piece to have some definite and trustworthy history in
regard to it.

It is an unusually good specimen of the style, and although pure Empire is at the same time characteristically American and could not have been made in
France. It is nowhere over-ornamented; its curves and
double curves are fine but restrained; its winged-claw
feet are without ornateness and are not tipped with
ormolu—a kind of brass much used by the French, and
very commonly on furniture feet, in the days of the
Empire. But to say that this sofa could not have been
made in France is not to say that it is better than the
French, for in the first years of the Empire style the
French made much of it very beautifully, although from
the first, there, the tendency toward grotesqueness was
more marked than it ever was with the American handling of the style.

But even here, Empire began very soon to tend
toward undesirability, and the table that is pictured, although it is without glaring faults, is illustrative of the

period when the style was just starting on its downward course but before the downward trend had gained much impetus.

Empire is readily recognisable, and for some not easily understood reason exercises a particular attraction upon most beginners in collecting. Indeed, most collectors go through a short period of Empire worship, after which some go to the other extreme of condemning it altogether.

Perhaps in its beginning the worship comes from the fascination of feet—the claw feet of Empire, which novices are apt to prefer to the far more desirable claw-and-ball of an earlier and better time.

And perhaps no better first rule can be given as to acquiring a knowledge of styles, than to learn definitely, simple though this is to the experienced, the difference between claw-foot and claw-and-ball—the claw-and-ball representing, it may almost be said, the Alpha of American furniture and claw-foot the Omega.

Following this, the beginner should learn to observe and distinguish accurately in regard to shapes in general: the shape and design of legs, the shape of desk-fronts and highboy tops, the shape of chair-backs, the fronts and the corners of chests of drawers. It is surprising how few, till they have trained themselves, can distinguish or describe, with any approach to clarity, the essential characteristics of a piece of old furniture.

That the terms Victorian and mid-Victorian are

synonymous with lack of grace and beauty is almost universally held to be a reproach upon that thus unfortunate Queen, as if it was she who was responsible; whereas the decline of style and shapes and beauty, in furniture and in other things, really began some years before the advent of Victoria, and was principally owing to the coming in of machinery and the machine-made product. Victoria does not seem to have stood personally for things beautiful, yet she ought not in fairness to be blamed for the inartistic influence of the march of progress. Similarly the taste and furniture of the reign of Louis Philippe are held in scorn in France.

In mentioning the names of the great founders of style—and there were really giants in those days—a name was omitted which, in the development of furniture, is greater than all: the name of Adam. For two brothers, Robert and James Adam, deeply influenced furniture-making—although they did not themselves make furniture!

They were architects, profoundly imbued with the best in ancient classic styles, the elder brother having spent several years in Italy and Dalmatia in study of the noble buildings of antiquity. The Adams designed buildings and rooms and the furniture for the rooms, and their sway was very powerful during the latter half of the eighteenth century. Chippendale's style and standards were established before they rose, but both

Heppelwhite and Sheraton were deeply influenced by them.

The brothers dictated not only the shape and size of rooms, the cornices, the windows, the doors, but everything within the rooms, in shapes and colours. As their fame increased, they led in the course and development of national taste.

These Scotchmen did fine work in London, notably the Adelphi buildings—the word meaning, as everybody knows, brothers, but, as very few know, really meant for the Adam brothers. Most of the houses that they built in London have disappeared or become office-buildings, but old-time illustrations, such as those by Stothard in "Sir Charles Grandison," show how beautiful Adam rooms can be.

And we personally had a pleasant experience, only last year, which gave us a close understanding of the Adams work. We were guests, in a house near Edinburgh, of which Robert Adam was the architect. The house itself was stately and dignified, yet without heaviness, and everything within it was a success; the exquisite oval dining-room, the library, with shelves and bookracks especially designed, the big and little delightful rooms, the ceilings, the cornices and mantelpieces and panelling that seemed to have grown with the house, and the exquisite furniture, much of which could, if seen separately, have passed as Sheraton and still more as the finest Heppelwhite.

Seeing this Adam house, still so beautifully maintained in its original condition, showed us, too, what absorbers of beauty Americans have always been, for there came to us memories of various old-time American homes of fine distinction, whose oval dining-rooms, charming pilasters, exquisite cornices, fanlights of great beauty, and furniture of delicate proportions and fine grace, we now understood were the direct result of the influence of the brothers Adam.   And in learning this we were more than ever realising what charm there is in a knowledge of periods and styles.

Some of these engravings illustrating Sir Charles Grandison are before us as we write, and they admirably set forth the beauty of Adam rooms.   Indeed, very much may be learned in regard to styles, from illustrations of old books, such as those of Fielding and Richardson, made by contemporaneous artists; and other eighteenth and early-nineteenth century illustrators of importance, beside Stothard, were Hoppner, Borel, Rooker, Downman and Rowlandson; this last name being best known to-day through his Doctor Syntax illustrations—pictures made for books written by the picturesque "Duke Coombs," and perpetuated on the widely known and valued Syntax blue china.

It is seldom, however, that modern illustrators of old-time books are anything but misleading; artists too often drawing with inaccuracy or from incorrect studio pieces; but illustrators of old-time furniture by a very few, such as Hugh Thomson and Brock, are thoroughly admirable.

Old-time paintings by artists who lived in the days of Chippendale or Heppelwhite or the Adams—and the best of the English portrait painters were of that century—are many of them of great interest to the old furniture lover from their accompaniments or backgrounds: and if anything is noticed that seems impossible or incongruous it may be deemed certain that there is some such excellent explanation to be found as that regarding the Italy-made portraits of the Izards.

CHAPTER III

THE CHARM OF ACCESSORIES

THE collector must study accessories, value accessories, use accessories. For in gathering into one's home the things of the past, it is the comparatively small acquisitions that count, quite as much as treasures that in themselves are of more size and importance. What is desired is a delightful atmosphere, a general effect, a charming old-time impression; and in the gaining of all this the accessories are of quite as much value as the things principal.

The fine old sideboard, the splendid high-boy, the fascinating tables and chairs, would be greatly wanting in effectiveness without the accompaniment of things of copper and brass, of glass and china, of pewter and silver and of Sheffield plate. There are candlesticks, fenders, andirons, kettles, jugs, salvers, peppershakers, clocks, pictures—the possibilities are endless.

There are houses rich in splendid antique possessions but entirely without atmosphere, houses that chill like a mere museum because attention has been given only to the big things, leaving the details unregarded; and there are houses in which things valuable from a money standpoint are few, but where there is a charmingly dominant impression of the old, because of attention to things that are small. One is tempted to believe, at times, that the little things are in reality the big ones.

A highly interesting corollary is that the gathering in of the old, and the giving to a home the atmosphere of the old, may be matter of far less expense than is generally supposed. It is a fine thing for a veritable lover of the antique to gain prizes at the cost of thousands of dollars, but it is also a fine thing that it is possible for the collector of limited means to secure in his home an effect that is charmingly complete and satisfactory. For the smaller antiques are to be found in very considerable number, and often for absurdly reasonable cost. At any moment one may happen upon a prize.

Chancing into Burlington, on the Delaware, just a few weeks ago, one of us picked up a fine specimen of old glass, a wine-glass, and all that was asked for it was twenty cents. That it was old was evident; how old was another question; and full examination at home pointed to about the year 1680, according to English authorities—which seemed too good to be true, although the "folded foot" certainly indicated an early date. We hesitated to believe in our own good fortune; "but," said a collecting friend to whom, with our admiration and doubts, we showed it, "do not forget that Burlington was settled in 1677, and that that was before the settlement of Philadelphia!"

There may be just as much of adventure and personal triumph in a fortunate find of the little as of the big; and it may be comparatively near by, like this glass, or it may be in some distant place. We found last year, in one of the most fascinating towns of fascinating Holland, ancient Dordrecht, a delectably shaped pepper of Sheffield plate, of about 1790. It is possible to know a great many of the dates of making shapes of Sheffield plate, from the ascertainable dates of similar shapes in solid silver, whose dates are known to the very year by their hall-marks; for most of the solid silver shapes were followed in Sheffield very shortly after being put on the market. Some designs lasted through quite a period, and others were produced for a short time only.

This high-standing pepper had been found in tearing down some old building, and an odd old, bright-eyed sailor, keeper of a canal-side ship-chandlery, had it. He wore earrings, showing him to be a native of northern Holland instead of Dordrecht, and on the morning we saw him, he and his wife were sweeping out of their house water that had been flooded in by a great storm overnight, the shop and the living-room adjacent being of exquisite neatness where the flood had not touched.

There was no doubt as to genuineness. The pepper was its own proof; that it was of Sheffield plate was in itself strong presumptive evidence to begin with, for the fine old process was long ago discontinued, and has only lately to some small degree been revived; and it had all the look and feel of age.

But even had there been reason to feel doubt, the price that the one-time sailor asked would have been proof of genuineness; for he wanted only two florins (eighty cents), and such a pepper could not be made and marketed for such a sum—this matter of price being often an excellent test as to true or imitation in cases where other tests are not absolutely convincing.

The pepper, thus a charming memento of a charming little adventure in an ancient town, was so corroded with age (another proof that it was genuine, for more money could have been asked had it been bright and clean) that it could not be polished; and so, although every lover of the old clings to his Sheffield even to shabbiness, for the plating in this process cannot be renewed, this was a case where the shabbiness was too great, and the worn Sheffield had to be covered by electroplate to make it possible for table use. Much as one may prize his Sheffield plate, it should be realised that, after all, it is only plating and not the article itself, and that what gave Sheffield plate its vogue and value was the beautiful shapes and admirable workmanship of most of the articles that were made by this process; for Sheffield plating was used during a period when charming shapes and excellent workmanship were the rule. But new plating does not destroy shape, it does not injure exquisite tooling; and as new Sheffield plate cannot be

FOUR OLD TEA CADDIES.

At the left, a Heppelwhite of about 1790; next is an Empire; the next is veneered with hare-wood and inlaid with satinwood; at the right, one of rosewood of 1835.

THE TWO OLD PEP-
PERS OF SHEF-
FIELD PLATE.

FOUR EXCELLENT TYPES OF OLD-TIME CANDLE LANTERNS, REMINDFUL OF THE DAYS OF PAUL REVERE AND THE "THREE O'CLOCK AND A CLOUDY MORNING" WATCHMAN.

THE DAVID AND GOLIATH STOVE-
PLATE, FOUND IN A JUNKMAN'S
WAGON. NOTE THE OLD GERMAN
DESCRIPTION OF THE FAMOUS SET-
TO.

A FIREBACK, SUCH AS WERE COM-
MONLY USED IN OLD FIREPLACES.
THEY WERE GENERAL IN AMERICA,
ALTHOUGH THIS PARTICULAR ONE
IS FROM FRANCE.

A FEW OLD TRIVETS, NECESSARILY THREE-LEGGED.

applied there should be no objection to having recourse to electroplating.

Sheffield plating was done by wiring thin plates of silver upon both sides of an oblong ingot of copper, and then heating them to adhesion in a furnace so arranged that its interior could be constantly watched, for at the moment of adhesion the silvered copper had to be drawn out or fusion would result; then, the wire removed, it was a matter of rolling to the desired thinness, without altering the proportion of relative thickness of silver and copper. Sheffield plating, therefore, could be done only with the raw material, and in a furnace, and could never be applied to a shaped article; and that is why it cannot be renewed when once worn off. Electroplating, on the contrary, is a process by which silver may be deposited upon a finished and shaped article by means of an electric current.

The pepper, an unusually good example of old-time style, is five inches high, rises from a round base, narrows above the base to a stem, then swells out, in a curve of marked distinction, in a circle a little larger than the base, and from this narrows gradually to a dome with a little point upon its top. The pepper shakes out of the sides of the dome. To a collector, the possession of a pair of an article of this sort, instead of only one, far more than doubles the value: and good fortune has given us another, of almost the identical period, and with just enough of difference to mark the general similarity and still further add to the value and interest, for the second pepper is only four and a half inches high, its dome has more of a curve, but the same odd pointed top, and the circle, immediately above the narrowing point, is of precisely the diameter of the circle of the base.

We put both peppers to their intended use, and this indicates, again, what we believe to be the true principle of collecting, which is that one should collect for his home only what his home needs, either for service or looks. Yet by this we mean nothing prosaic or too practical, for use may consist in looking beautiful, as with a picture or a piece of china, as well as in answering an actual need. One of the finest characters in all fiction, Bishop Myriel, remarked, one day, that "The beautiful is as useful as the useful," and then added, thoughtfully—"more so, perhaps."

If we go into details, as with these old peppers, in regard to sizes and shapes, and methods of manufacture, and problems and decisions, it is with the hope of thus suggesting to others what discoveries may be made, what questions may be met, what difficulties may be solved. And if, throughout, we tell much of what we personally have done or experienced, it is only because we wish to show that others may do much the same and that many may do more; and if we tell of actual finds it is only to encourage others to be ready to see and seize opportunities.

And as to prices—everything cannot be bought cheaply, but what a genuine joy it is to discover a treasure by yourself, recognise its interest, and secure it— without meanness!—from some one who does not care for it, or is at least glad for you to have it!

There is a kind of collecting that is more like hoarding, like that of the man who stores a hundred and sixty pewter dishes out of sight in a dark closet; or the other man who has hidden two hundred old candlesticks in his attic, where neither he nor any one else ever sees them; or the one who has packed away masses of cupplates; or him of the forty-nine stored-away firebacks, who feels embittered if he hears that even one has been acquired by any other collector! The fine, free flavor of true collecting is lost to him who hoards to hide; and also there is a distinct selfishness in keeping from others many a possibility of acquisition.

As to firebacks (which are flat plates of iron to protect the back walls of fireplaces and at the same time throw more heat into the room), we have one from France, and bearing the royal arms and motto, which was discovered opportunely and secured by patience, and at which royal toes must often have been warmed.

That we actually waited for this fireback, this reredos, for six years after discovering it in an out-of-the-way corner, adds greatly to its personal charm to us; and it may be encouraging to mention this long wait, to show beginners not only that they should not be disappointed by not securing everything without delay, but that an enforced waiting for something known and desired may give an added desirability and a keener joy.

And one need not go to France for prizes; even firebacks may be discovered nearer home. There is an old unoccupied Colonial Governor's mansion of the early seventeen hundreds, not many miles from where we live, that has treasure for some one some day. It is a panelled and corniced and fireplaced old mansion, and the poetically inclined dreamer can hear the tap-tapping of the Governor's heels and the soft murmur of silken gowns. To him it would be cruel to say that it is but the water in the cellar floating old butter crocks against the floor! Lovely the old place has been—and it had fine firebacks; six of them—now stored for safe keeping in a near-by farmhouse closet!

And there are others! Six or seven months ago a junkman's wagon moved slowly up a road a half-mile from our house. It was heavy with uninteresting heterogeneousness, but a rusty bit of iron peeping over the edge of the wagon-box called for examination.

The driver stopped his horse. The rusty piece of iron was drawn out, and the inquiry was made: "How much?"

Till that moment the iron had been to the junkman merely junk; now it suddenly assumed some value: "A dollar and a half."

And it was gladly purchased, for it was an old

"Pennsylvania Dutch stove-plate," though made long before the time of stoves, with raised figures of Goliath and David, and an inscription, in old-time German, giving some particulars of their famous set-to.

As the possession of accessories is as important as that of larger things, so is their proper placing as important. Always and everywhere, with things little or big, there ought to be the right thing in the right place. We have a friend in a flat who keeps six pairs of brass andirons under his hall table, and although they are funny there they are certainly not effective.

There is an old desk in our upper hall, and it illustrates the possible co-ordination of principal and accessories, for we have given it an old pewter ink-well, and hung above it an engraving by Warner of Henry Clay. That this engraving was given us by a grandson of Warner suggests other possibilities of interesting association. The desk stands between two deep-silled windows, and the wall-paper is a plain little stripe of that *café au lait* colour so commonly used in Colonial days. In front of the desk is one of the old-fashioned braided rugs still made in some of our country towns. Everything in the hall is similarly in accord, and on top of the desk stand a pair of eighteenth century brass candlesticks, of pedigree personally known to us, of the kind that slide up and down, so as to be either short or tall— a kind often seen in silver but seldom in brass.

There should never be crowding. The aim should

be at comparatively little rather than at too much—although just enough is better still.   And how to know when just enough has been reached is matter for constant study and observation.

There are houses where precious things are so crowded and cluttered that one looks about in dismay; it is as if a man were to wear two or three hats!   If there is too much, get rid of the unnecessary.   Start an attic for your grandchildren.   Or give the not-needed pieces to some young collector.   Do something!   Don't keep a clutter!

If there are too few antiques to furnish the house, it is better to furnish one room at a time.   It is a great mistake to muddle new things and old.   The effect is distressing, and the value of the scattered antiques is largely lost.

Pictures are among the important accessories of old furniture, and they may properly be engravings and etchings, paintings and water-colours, old prints—the variety is wide.   But the most interesting point is that it is not really necessary, for effectiveness and harmony, that the pictures be old.   An excellent picture of any period almost always harmonises with excellent furniture.

A play by Arnold Bennett represents three periods, a quarter of a century apart from each other, but the entire action takes place in one room—a room in which the furniture, the floor covering, the wall treatment, the lighting fixtures, the mantelpiece, change with each period, showing for each the average good taste of the time. Even the pictures change—all but one, a large landscape, apparently meant to represent a Ruysdael or Hobbema. Through all the mutations of fashion in furnishing, this painting remains the only thing un-altered, the only thing that harmonises with all the periods.

The general subject of accessories is almost endless in its possibilities, for there are accessories in every possible line.

There are old-time lanterns still to be found, and they can be hung to advantage on porches or at side en-trances; and they can readily be adjusted for electric lights. Being outdoor articles, they seem to look much more at home out-of-doors than they would in an interior. Our four, obtained from time to time at various American places, are all of excellent proportions and design; and one, with a little column at each corner, is very unusual in being all of wood, except for the little metal crown in the centre and the glass; another, en-tirely without glass, is of perforated tin, painted black, and at night glows through its patterned punches with brilliant, glimmering success. These are excellent ex-amples of the lanterns used a century ago, and are sug-gestive of Paul Revere and the "Half past three and a cloudy morning" of the old-time watchman.

Tea-caddies are another of the delightful minor pursuits, and reward by their delicate workmanship and widely different shapes. One, taperingly coffer-shaped, that stands on the sideboard, is of beautiful mahogany, is an exquisite bit of cabinet work, and is really a miniature copy of an ancient Roman type of chest. Of the others, only one is used for tea, and this is kept with a tea-set, the other two standing on broad window-sills and serving as useful household boxes. These tea-caddies must all have been made with prideful workmanship, for there is delicate inlay with satinwood and harewood, and little compartments heedfully wrought, and ivory buttons for lifting little interior covers—and all have keys, for these were luxurious holders of a luxury; for tea used to be very dear. And what a contrast to the unlovely tea-holders, of japanned tin, set forth as the offering of this twentieth century!

Old tea-caddies are much more readily found in England than in America, as the use of tea has so long been general among all classes. Yet fine ones are by no means hopelessly scarce on this side of the water; and a letter arrived only a few weeks ago, from one of the Southern States, saying:

"Will you please tell me what I have found? It is a little box in the shape of a doll's trunk and there is an ivory shield around the key hole—inside is a partition and two square pieces of wood with tiny brass knobs in the centre of each that fit on top of each side of the partition. I never saw anything like it before."

A GROUP OF LITTLE MIRRORS; 1 AND 5 ARE OF A TYPE MADE ABOUT
1750 AND LATER, IN MANY DIFFERENT SIZES; 4 IS EXQUISITE HEP-
PELWHITE; 3 IS EMPIRE.

OLD LITTLE TABLES; OFTEN CALLED TRIPOD TABLES.

1 (At left) Rimmed square top; can be traced back to 1740.

2 Rimmed tip-table; unusually good snake feet; at least as old as 1750.

3 Candlestand; a type of a century ago.

4 Mahogany tea-table; snake-footed; with rimmed top that both twirls and tips.

5 Empire style; about 1815; once had a rim, which was planed off for convenience of card-players.

6 A kind often used as a fire-screen.

7 Hexagon top, old but not fine.

Among accessories, little tables are of importance. Naturally enough, tables are usually classed among principals, but little ones justly come under the head of accessories. And it is an alluring search, for there is such variety of shape and design. Scarcely is it possible to find two little tables precisely alike; and always there is some corner where one of these may stand, usefully or ornamentally or both. One may be at the head of each bed, for candle, matches, watch or water; one may stand near the library fire, ready to hold the newspaper or the casual magazine or book; one may be ready for the tea-tray or the coffee after dinner; one may be ready for spools and scissors; one may hold flowers at the window—the possible uses are multitudinous. You will never quit acquiring little tables!

The most sought-for and rarest of little tables is the "pie-crust" tip-table, so named from its apparently finger-dented pie-crust-like margin of regular irregularity. Always rare, it has practically disappeared from collecting possibility, yet we discovered one last spring, not particularly valued by its owners, kept without care, pushed carelessly about and in shabby condition, but impossible of acquisition because of the red-tape of an orphanage board!

But there are still delightful tables to find, with feet and legs of infinite variety, with tops round or square or hexagon, tops that turn and tip, tops smooth or with the much-prized rim—and the old-time method of making a rim-top was, always, not to apply a rim as a separate piece, but to make rim and top in one piece, out of the same thick board, thus excellent being the artisanship of the past.

It is a far too common error, to aim only at collecting the larger articles and to ignore the small ones except such as are kept in trays or drawers, like cameos, samplers, snuffboxes, fans, beadbags, pinchbeck, fobs. It is one of the greatest mistakes to ignore the smaller articles that are kept in sight as actual accessories.

How much more impressive and beautiful is a fireplace if it has old fire irons and a trivet—delightful name!—and if the mantelshelf holds a pair of old candlesticks and a clock of old and good design! How delightful is the ancient four-poster that is outfitted with valance of dimity and white quilted cover, and which has beside it a good braided rug! What charm is added to an old-time dining-table if the table service has sufficient of the old, in glass and china and silver, to carry out the old-time impression! And how much the fascination of an ancient cupboard is added to if it is filled with china of the past! Charles Lamb wrote that, when he went a-visiting, his first inquiry was always for the china-cupboard.

CHAPTER IV

THE CHARM OF FINDS NEAR HOME

IT is a positive delight to find antiques near home. It gives such a comfortable, satisfactory sort of pleasure to feel that you have but to step out of the house, this very day, and find some prize! There is immense charm in the possession of treasures that you have had for years, immense charm in the possession of finds that you have made hundreds or even thousands of miles away; but a charm of a different, a delightful, and an encouraging kind is in the sensation of discovering something near at hand, and securing it, and at a reasonable price. If you can find things near home you can find them anywhere!

Such a fillip of a find was ours but a few days ago. The possibility was first come upon early last fall, when one of us happened into a notary's office, a mile or so from home, for attestation of signature. It was a modern house, without the slightest suggestion of containing anything of the past; for it is among the things that the lover of the old must learn, that the unpromising house may yield a prize, just as the promising house may dispense disappointment. But the collector must be ready at any moment to find a find!

Immediately upon entering the office, a little table was noticed; it was almost hidden under a typewriter and scattered papers but it was clear that it was an exquisite Heppelwhite. A little of the inlay had gone, but on the whole it was in admirable condition. So much was apparent at a glance.

The table was duly praised. It really belonged to the notary's wife, so it appeared, who had been given it a dozen years before, by an old lady of almost eighty, who had inherited it. But without this pedigree, it was clear that it was a table of between 1780 and 1790. No offer was made for it; a direct offer to buy, when the owner has expressed no desire to sell, is almost certain to offend, and to spoil possibilities, even although the owner may in reality be anxious to dispose of what he has. But there is always some way to get around this, if the piece is at all buyable; in general the best method is to ask if the owner knows of any similar thing, elsewhere, that might be obtained. The difference may seem slight, but in results it is very great, for it gives the owner a chance to sell without losing pride—and the pride of a private owner is a precarious thing!

Of course there was no other similar table to tell of; but perhaps, suggested the wife, she might be willing, some day—she hesitated—after all, this was used only as a typewriter-stand—

Whereupon, an offer of fifteen dollars was at once made; and a few weeks later—just before the Christmas

THE EXQUISITE HEPPELWHITE TABLE FOUND IN A COUNTRY
NOTARY'S OFFICE.

THE MOST DESIRABLE TYPE OF FOUR POSTER; A SHERATON WITH
SLENDER FLUTED POSTS.

last past—there came a telephone inquiry: Did we still care for that table? And within an hour it was in our house, for such an opportunity (and such a table!) should instantly be seized.

It is a dainty, delicate, delightful Heppelwhite, of the beautiful tawny mahogany that ruled before the San Domingo, with its fire and glow, appeared and won supremacy.

It is twenty-nine inches high, and that it is oval, instead of round, adds to its value and distinction. Its top is forty-two inches by thirty-one, thus making a delectable curve.

The legs are square-sided and tapering, with a band of inlay around each, near the bottom. But there is inlay along the sides of each leg as well—inlay in delicate threads—and there are inlaid oval medallions at the top and outer sides of each leg, and inlay lines around the entire top of the table, and inlay is minutely wrought, with infinite skill and delicacy, upon the drawer fronts.

The oval medallions at the tops of the legs are of satinwood, and of satinwood is the larger oval medallion in the centre of the drawer, which is four inches by two, and made of sixteen triangles of satinwood, which ray to the centre, and whose outer edges curve against tiny inlays of ebony; all being enclosed within two delicate lines, one of ebony and one of holly. But even more delicate, even more amazing is the work upon the border extending around each drawer front; a border precisely seven-sixteenths of an inch in width, but comprising seven distinct lines of inlay. The outside line is of mahogany, laid at right angles to the mahogany of the principal surface of the drawer; then comes a thread of holly; the third line is made in unusual fashion, of tiny pieces of alternate ebony and satinwood, laid diagonally with exquisite skill and daintiness and containing four hundred and sixty separate pieces of wood!—such being the patient and devoted skill of old-time artisans who loved their work. Next is a slender line of what seems harewood; a line of golden brown with greenish tinge; and then comes satinwood, in a narrow band so laid as to show, on minute inspection, that it is at right angles to the grain; then another thread of the delicate harewood; and, last of all, another line of satinwood laid with its length with the grain.

Enclosing all, is a sixteenth of an inch of mahogany beading; the lines of beading and inlay together, with infinite wealth of workmanship, occupying precisely a half an inch of width.

And with all this, such being the art of the maker, there are reserve, restraint, delicacy of effect, complete absence of gaudiness, a soft symphony of tawny and brown.

It is delightful possibilities such as this that add tang and zest, relish and savour, to the charming joy of gathering the old; finds that are personal triumphs, as all finds ought to be, but which have a flavour all their own when made near home.

And the possession of even a single piece of exquisite and restrained workmanship not only raises the standard of a collection but tends to maintain one's own standard of distinction and is a constant lesson in good taste.

The subject of inlay is one of constant fascination. It was considerably used by the artisans of Europe, even as far back as some centuries ago, and the intarso work of Italy, such as seen in sixteenth-century choir stalls, and the Holland insets of tulips and leaves of the seventeenth century, are notable, as well as the inlay of the French of the time of Louis the Fourteenth—which was really much more overlay than inlay as can be seen in much of the work of Boulle existing to this day. But inlay in narrow lines, as it is known in things that may be gathered to-day, may for practical purposes be said to be a thing of the late seventeen hundreds, after the passing of Chippendale influence.

And there are so many things to learn in regard to the tiny but effective differences!—for example, that satinwood and holly are both pale yellow, but that satinwood has an exquisite satiny grain, with tiny markings, whereas holly has beauty of colour without beauty of wood, and that, therefore, holly was held to be excellent for threads of inlay and satinwood for broader bands and surfaces. The exquisite work of Heppelwhite was exquisitely imitated by the best American artisans, but there was many a worker, especially in our smaller towns, who secured Heppelwhite effects by the use of American curly maple and mahogany, instead of with satinwood and harewood and ebony. And all inlay that seems to be ebony may not be ebony; for dear old White of Selborne tells of digging up bog oak, "as black as ebony," and very ponderous, and that it was to quite an extent used in cabinet work as inlay with whiter woods.

That the total existing supply of old furniture is less than it was is inevitable; but a much more important fact is that it is still very large. And the reason why it is still large is that, a century ago, every one of a million houses in America contained furniture that is now sought for as desirable and excellent. A century ago, in the million houses, there were millions of excellent chairs, for there were many in each house; there were millions of chests of drawers; there were many million pieces of pewter and silver and glass. Much of this immense total of the past has been worn out, thrown away, burned, lost, gathered into museums, but much remains, still possible of acquisition. And, as with the Heppelwhite table, many a specimen not acquirable to-day will be acquirable to-morrow, from change of fancy, from the breaking up of a family, from one or another of various possible reasons.

It is not only in the Eastern States that old things

are to be secured, although the greatest part are there. In early days, thousands and thousands of families moved westward, taking their household belongings with them, in wagons and flatboats, or even around the Horn, and good old things may be picked up in a host of places—may be picked up anywhere. A novel by one of our foremost authors represents a home on the Pacific Coast, in the Northwest, of some seventy-five years ago, as being full of what we now call antique and Colonial. And, as just one concrete example of the present day, we may mention a Seattle family who have, in their dining-room, a Sheraton sideboard, some Chippendale chairs, some pieces of Empire, and also old glass and silverware. We have personally come upon obtainable antiques in quite a number of States besides those of the East; and as all collectors are "from Missouri, and want to know," it may be added that the chief treasure of Tom Sawyer was the brass knob from an andiron—showing thus that antiques are findable in Missouri!

All of which shows that any one, no matter where his home is, may hope to find at least something, not far away from it. It is really astonishing how antiques have scattered.

A collecting friend went not long ago on a business errand to a grist-mill. The owner was not in the office, and in search of him our friend went to the top floor. There, in a corner, practically thrown away, stood a superb old extension-table of the finest San Domingo mahogany; a table that, by means of a sort of rope-managed cantilever, slides out to almost unbelievable length. The table was bought, and very reasonably. That was in Pennsylvania; and just a few months ago an Ohio friend came upon a superb Sheraton sideboard shoved out of the way and forgotten in a disused ice-house, where shortly it would have rotted away or been broken up. It was bought for eight dollars; the owner hastily realising that what he had deemed worthless was worth something, and putting what he deemed a high price upon it.

And within a fortnight a letter has come to us, telling of the unexpected find, in a basement in a Colorado town, of a veritable block-front chest of drawers—one of the rarest of old-fashioned things.

In gathering for the furnishing of a house, one looks not only for the large things but the small, not only for the elaborate but the simple; for all have an influence in making the desired atmosphere.

Recently we were passing a toll-gate house, less than half an hour from home, when a big brown jar of excellent shape was noticed, stuck wrong-side up on the picket of a fence. The toll-gate keeper did not want it—a jar upon the picket's rim was but a simple jar to him, and it was nothing more—and said that a quarter would overpay him. It proved to be what it had seemed, in that moment's glance: early American pottery. It is lead-glazed, with a silvery glimmer on a deep seal brown.

We already possessed another specimen of this same ware, found in the cellar of our own house when we bought it; a narrow-necked jug of the same soft brown, and very shapely. A third specimen of this very ware, came still more oddly. For at an auction in a house within easy distance of ours, a large jar was put up; a thing absurd of aspect, for every inch was covered with gaudy flowers varnished upon it in the fashion of thirty years ago. But there was somehow a suggestion of what it really was, and a five cents' bid secured it. A day's soaking in a laundry-tub took off the offending pictures and the jar stands in the simple dignity of its plain finish and excellent lines.

And we have a fourth jar of early American work, not so old as the other three, but also found near home— this last being grey with cobalt-blue markings, and showing distinctly a Chinese influence in shape, the trade with China being of great importance in early American days. The four jars range in height from twelve to eighteen inches.

A delightful old chest, extremely interesting in its home-made decorations, was a happy near-by find. It is a wedding chest, and the man who made it, probably the bridegroom himself, lettered upon it laboriously a motto that one does not expect from the proverbial phlegm of his people, the "Pennsylvania Dutch"; for it is *"Lieben und nicht haben ist härtter den Aangraben"* —which is to say, that to love and not to possess is worse than the grave!—assuredly a proper warmth of sentiment for the bride to recognise.

And over in New Jersey, on a little trip one day, we came upon an empty and deserted house, on a cedar-bordered road, on a low-rising ridge. The doors and the windows had disappeared; there seemed nothing but wavering walls and feeble floors and shaky stair—but the stair was mountable, and led to a room in which stood a chest, an oak chest, iron-bound, and very old, and very heavy. And it was locked!

The owner of the deserted house lived not far away, and he came and looked at the chest. "I forgot all about it," he said. "Just take it along."

"But it's heavy—and it's full!"

"Ah!"—and he grappled with it—and lifted the sides and top, leaving the bottom on the floor, deserted and broken, and covered with a clattering mass of bits of old iron, the savings of some one for many years. But the panelled sides and the top, with the antique iron bands and ancient lock and wrought-iron handles, made a good-looking chest, that merely needed a new bottom.

And lest, again, we should seem, with chests or with anything else, to be telling of experiences that could not generally happen, we may mention a friend in Philadelphia who is the possessor of an old chest of camphor-wood, with Chinese markings, that was obtained for very

AN OLD "DUTCH DOOR," TRANS-
PLANTED FROM AN OLD
HOUSE.

JARS OF EARLY AMERICAN MAKE.

1 The jar found on the toll-
gate fence.

2 Found in a cellar.

3 Shows Chinese influence.

4 From an auction; gaudy flowers were pasted all over it.

WEDDING CHEST, OF THE "PENNSYLVANIA DUTCH"; WITH A MOTTO OF GRIM SENTIMENT.

THE OLD OAK CHEST, IRON BOUND AND PANELED.

little at a storage-warehouse that had kept it for many years and had lost all track of its owner. Another chest, in a home near by, which was left to its owner by a neighbour's will, is covered all over with fine red morocco-like leather, bound at the edges with brass, studded with brass nails, and tooled with gold. Nothing is definitely known of its origin, but it is reputed to be Spanish, and looks the part.

In every direction, and for every collector, there are all sorts of acquisitions possible near home.

Among our own finds are three long, old settees, that were part of the furnishing of an old-time little lecture-hall, rich in the memories of Emerson and Garrison, and of gatherings still earlier. The building was in process of destruction, and it was merely a matter of mentioning that three settees could be used to advantage to have them turned over to us. Two or three other folks got two or three more—and the rest were destroyed.

Each of our three is placed in some carefully selected location; one at either end of the rear porch, and the third under a bank of windows, where it seems almost part of the design of the house.

A highly interesting line of collecting is that of old-time things which can be built into the very structure of the house and add materially to the general old-time effect; as, in our own case, an old and very broad Dutch door made so as to permit of opening the upper half if so desired, without opening the lower.   It was got from an old house in course of demolition and was built into the library, in place of a door that was narrow and inadequate of aspect.

When there came to us, from separate sources, two table-legs of Empire design, they fitted admirably into the scheme of constructing a much-needed china closet, for, sawed down the middle, they made two pairs of pilasters for the cupboard sides, and look as if they had always been there.

Probably our very oldest belonging came to us from less than two miles away, and within the past year, and for ten cents!   It is a joint stool.   Nobody cared for it, nobody knew anything about it.   The household belongings of an old Quaker family were being disposed of and here was this heavy oak joint stool: four-legged, square-sided, low-braced, somewhat broader at the bottom than at the top, and over two hundred years old.

Joint stools were common in the days before chairs became common; joint stools and benches.   For chairs are almost a modern innovation, so far as general use of them is concerned, which, broadly speaking, did not come till the eighteenth century.   The King James' version nowhere refers to a chair, and Shakespeare, although he uses the word, uses it as meaning a chair of state or ceremony, or a Sedan-chair.   It is probable that there is not a line in his works with any reference to chairs as household articles of ordinary use.   There

used to be chairs, or thrones, for kings, and chairs of
state for peers, and a chair for the head of a house; and
the expression "taking the chair" perpetuates the old-
time sense of distinction and exclusiveness.

After chairs began to come in, joint stools were for
quite a while also used, the use of the two overlapping
until that of chairs became general; Dick Steele somewhere writes of Colley Cibber that he had a hair-trunk
and two or three joint stools in his room; and this stool
that we acquired is of the period when joint stools were
vanishing. It is of oak and is an extremely interesting
survival and a marked rarity.

But one often comes across odd misapprehensions.
We know a Frenchman, a collector of Henry II—the
way a Frenchman rumbles out Ah-ri doo is a delight—
who had three joint stools, not so very different from
the one we have ourselves, and he vowed they were
dwarfs' tables, and when we sought to dissuade him
from that belief he only affirmed that there must have
been three dwarfs, and not one dwarf only, who owned
three tables!

As to wood in furniture: after the introduction of
mahogany, early in the eighteenth century, that was
deemed the most precious wood in both England and
America, though in both countries much excellent and
beautiful furniture was made of other woods, such as
walnut. Maple, curly maple, cherry and apple were
also used by cabinet-makers in this country, but oak

never obtained here anything like its popularity in England. In France, which has always held itself as a nation apart in matters of taste, mahogany never attained the vogue it won in England and America, and very much of the finest French furniture is of walnut, French walnut, however, being different from the walnut of America and easily distinguishable. So that it must by no means be thought that mahogany has the monopoly of beauty or excellence.

A fine and dignified article of walnut should be preferred to the same article in inferior workmanship or design but of mahogany. But merely because, at times, one sees mahogany furniture that is far from the best, there should never be the slightest belittling of the finest mahogany, with its capacity for splendid polish and its deep, dark glow.

One does not readily think of apartment dwellers in New York finding antiques near home—except in the antique shops—but one day when we were ourselves apartment-dwellers there, the janitor, who was repairing a lock, noticed that we had old-time furniture and said, all in one sentence: "I've got an old table down in the basement and it's got lion's feet and eagle's wings on the legs and my wife wants me to burn it up to get it out of the way and I'll give it to you for a dollar."

That was quite enough for the risking of a dollar, and in a few moments the table was in our apartment —a fine example of early Empire, and of superb mahogany. When we were moving, not long afterward, it and other things were crated by a dealer, accustomed to handle such things for shipment, and he offered fifty dollars for the table, now polished and fine, taking the actual money from his pocket as additional temptation; but it seemed that although there would be other chances to obtain fifty dollars, we might never again have such a table offered us under like circumstances.

Another excellent table is one whose top both tips and turns, and which has unusually good snake-feet and well-proportioned pedestal. It dates back to about 1730 or 1750, cost us eight dollars, and is another of our near-at-home acquisitions, as is also a small tip-and-turn table of the same age, that was sold us for three dollars by some one who did not care for such things.

We have had several interesting experiences with old four-posters; one, that we found in the garret of a house near our then home in New York State, is a field-bed of slender Heppelwhite design, with graceful curving canopy. Four-posters are more commonly found nowadays in America than in England, and for much less money.

It may help some who do not readily find the things they want, if we say that we have not as yet picked up precisely the four-poster for which we have long looked—that best of all kinds of bed, the Sheraton, with posts slender and fluted. There are several that we know of, near home, not at present obtainable, but precisely like one recently bought by a fortunate friend for eight dollars; and our own time is sure to come, although probably for not quite so low a price. There would be neither satisfaction nor triumph in collecting if results were all easy and quick.

Although so many things are to be found near home by the lover of the antique, it is of no use to find them if the finder doesn't appreciate what he finds. A few months ago, calling upon acquaintances who had newly moved into their home, they spoke, rather vaguely, of liking old furniture, and had two or three pieces. "But we particularly wanted an old corner-cupboard, and as we had to have a cupboard of some kind, we bought this" —pointing to a modern thing of birch, built topplingly, as so many modern cupboards are, with ignorance of the laws of construction.

We had noticed, as we motored over, that in the corner of the porch of the combined country post-office, store, and home, stood a capacious, double-doored corner-cupboard, of fine and dignified lines; in evident need of restoration, but only of restoration that could easily be made with small expense. We spoke of this corner-cupboard, adding that as it was out-of-doors it could probably be readily bought.

"Oh—that! We found that in this house when we moved in, and gave it to the postmaster!"

CHAPTER V

THE CHARM OF FINDS FROM FAMOUS PLACES

A FRIEND of ours has an old secretary, with tall cupboard space above and drawers below; a desk prized for its age and its associations, for in Revolutionary times it was part of the furnishing of the Chew Mansion; the fine old stone house, still standing and still occupied by the Chews, about which centred the Battle of Germantown; the house which, held as a fort by British soldiers, made such successful resistance to Washington's attacks as to decide the day adversely to the Colonial cause.

A descendant Chew took the desk, long after the war, to his office in Philadelphia, and, retiring from professional life, gave it to a lawyer friend. By him it was taken home, to be given over to his children to be marred and marked, and then taken to his own law office; and on his death it was easily obtained by its present owner, who has it in his home in a suburban town.

Thus can be followed the movements of a pedigreed piece that has never known the hands of a dealer but which has been held in careless estimation until its present ownership. And how fortunate it is, for collectors who value fine old things and especially things from famous places, that the owners who happen not to feel interest in their own precious belongings are so often willing to let them go into proper hands!

The years that the old desk spent in lawyers' offices is a reminder, too, of the old treasure not infrequently to be found, especially in the smaller towns, in the offices of lawyers, doctors and real estate men. Many an old desk and table has drifted to such a destination.

There is no place in America more justly famous than Independence Hall, and no furniture more precious to Americans than the chairs used by the Signers, as members of the Continental Congress, when they voted for the Declaration of Independence. These chairs were long ago permitted to get into private ownership, and the greater number of those that now stand in the old assembly room of the Congress, and which are firmly believed to be veritable, have been given or loaned by their modern owners.

Yet even a chair of a Signer may drift near you in unappreciated ownership. Quite recently, one of us was calling at a Philadelphia home when another caller entered; a man, a member of one of the old local families. His eye was at once taken with a chair of old-fashioned shape, and he asked about it with interest.

"That is one of two chairs, made from an old elm that used to stand in front of Independence Hall," he was told. "The chairs are exact reproductions of the

THE OLD DESK, FROM THE LORD STIRLING MANSION, IN A SETTING
THAT HARMONIZES.

A TALL OLD HIGHBOY, FROM MARYLAND; AN ADMIRABLE EXAMPLE, SHOWING THE BEST POINTS OF THIS FINE TYPE, IN GENERAL SHAPE, CORNERS, LEGS, BONNET-TOP, AND HANDLES.

A SMALL AND SIMPLE HIGHBOY, SLENDER AND GRACEFUL, OF REMARK-ABLY FINE LINES; ABOUT 1750.

Signers' chairs, and each was given by the mayor to a representative citizen. Some years ago this chair changed hands and came to us."

"Oh—"; the Philadelphian was interested, absorbed, engrossed in thought and examination;—"so that's like a Signers' chair!"

"Yes; and I suppose you have seen the originals used by the Continental Congress who signed the Declaration."

"No!" eagerly. "Where are they? In Carpenters' Hall, I suppose?"

"No," was the patient reply, while an amused twinkle was apparent; "they are in Independence Hall; where they signed, you know."

"Oh, yes, of course! Where they signed. That's why they were called the Signers—eh!—" He beamed in triumph at his own acumen. "Do you know, I was told that among the old furniture that I inherited two years ago from Aunt Mary there was a chair of a Signer —Several of my ancestors were mixed up in the Revolution, you know, and there really is a chair that looks just like that." He beamed again. "So I have a Signers' chair," he said, complacently, and with no more of a collector's or patriotic thrill than as if he had inherited a new pattern of ironing-board.

Naturally, one goes from one Revolutionary memory to another; and there comes the thought of the old-time house that was once the home of that picturesque Revolutionary general and claimant of an earldom, known as Lord Stirling. For he had a mansion, set in the midst of a thousand acres in a New Jersey region of hills and pleasant plains; a region still as attractive and delightful as ever. The house still stands, but has been quite altered from its old-time aspect, even the great old chimneys having been replaced by chimneys meagre and small.

It would seem impossible to obtain there anything of the old; and yet we found that the house still held a few old treasures, among them being a desk, of apple-wood, with inlay of holly and black wood; a desk with fifteen little drawers where usually there are pigeon holes; and this desk the owner was ready quite reasonably to sell.

Even if the desk was not owned by Stirling himself, it is a fine specimen, of undoubted age—it was made about 1780 or a little later—and coming from the house of such a distinguished historical figure possesses in high degree the charm that attaches to things from famous places. And it may possibly enough have belonged personally to Stirling, who died in 1783; only one has a far more satisfactory feeling if he claims only when he is positive; and there are possible positive finds sufficient in number to satisfy even the most ambitious collector.

The desk is of the slant-top kind, and could be of considerably earlier date, if judged only by its general shape and its straight-edged bracket feet, than 1780, but the free use of inlay, especially around the interior drawers, marks it as being not earlier than this. It is of the Heppelwhite school, and apparently of American make; the adaptable American spirit having made it by using simple applewood of the fine tawny hue so loved by Heppelwhite personally; had it been made in England it might date back to about 1775, styles on this side of the ocean usually following those of the other side with somewhat of leeway, thus requiring a little later dating.

The slant-top was the earliest kind of desk, desks being in origin portable writing-boxes placed on frames with four legs. Such desks are still to be found and are to be highly prized when standing on legs that are cabriole or bandy—the two terms being interchangeable. Then the idea must have dawned upon cabinet makers to incorporate a slant-top with a chest of drawers, and thus there came about the slant-top secretary that ranged from 1730 to nearly the last of the eighteenth century, through ball feet and claw-and-ball, bracket feet and feet with ogee curve. In the 1790's cabinet makers had another inspiration and evolved a kind of desk without slant-top; a desk which, when closed, resembled a chest of drawers but, instead of having drawers which were graduated from the deepest at the bottom to the shallowest at top, apparently had the deepest drawer at top. On drawing this out a clever set of brass quadrants allowed the front of the apparent drawer to descend as a writing surface. Throughout a large part of the eighteenth century, secretaries or desks, with drawers below and bookcase or cabinet above, were in use, and they have persisted well down to our own time, but have seldom appealed to the most discriminating taste. An admirable kind of desk was made by Sheraton, with big flat top, and drawers down each side, and ample knee space; desks which were models of comfort and of beauty and were largely used by men of large affairs, whether statesmen or business men; such a desk was personally used by President Washington and can still be seen in the beautiful old city hall of New York.

The entire matter of desks is full of interest, with many a problem and surprise; perhaps the greatest of all surprises being that a superb desk of Louis the Fifteenth, in the Louvre and known as the *"bureau de roi,"* has a roll-top that looks like the roll-tops of desks in modern business offices, with the difference that the king's roll-top went back out of sight in a rigid curve instead of with the separate slats of to-day.

The old desk from Lord Stirling's house was thoroughly looked over for secret drawers, there being so many places about an old desk where secret compartments may be. The location of secret places can be determined by comparing outside measures with the measures of drawers and cubbyholes and allowing for

LIBRARY FIREPLACE; WITH FIRE-IRONS AND BRASSES FROM FAMOUS PLACES. THE FIRESIDE CHAIR IS FROM THE EASTERN SHORE OF MARYLAND.

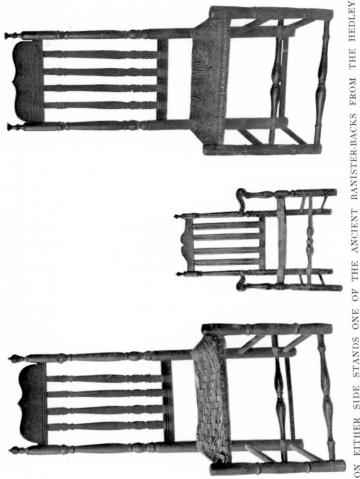

ON EITHER SIDE STANDS ONE OF THE ANCIENT BANISTER-BACKS FROM THE HEDLEY GARRET. IN THE CENTER IS AN ANCIENT BANISTER-BACK ARM CHAIR.

thickness of wood. If there is space unaccounted for it means that there is probably a secret drawer. Very often the secret drawer is hidden beside the compartment that, in almost every old desk, is in the centre of the pigeonholes; a compartment which held the inkwell or the decanter according to the taste of the owner! Oftentimes this entire compartment draws forward, disclosing a hiding place behind; once in a while a desk was so made that two decorative pillars, at either side of the compartment, were drawn out on the release of a secret spring, disclosing a book-shaped hollow for hiding letters or papers; still more difficult to find (unless it shows the knife marks of decades of investigators) is the secret opening in the writing surface, about where the inkwell stands. Such an opening is sometimes accidentally discovered by pressing upon one end of the wood that covers it, and thus disclosing a space in which a few papers could be hidden, almost within the thickness of the wood. Secret places in desks were very useful to our ancestors, who had no safety-deposit boxes to depend on. A secret drawer adds greatly to the interest of any desk, and should always be carefully sought for.

Naturally and appropriately, the value of things antique is added to by association with places of historical note; and it is surprising how much this feature of collecting is neglected, in spite of the possibilities it holds.

Take ancient Amsterdam, for example—why, we

found that we could get there either a nose for a bellows, or a block-front chest of drawers, or the gable-
front of an ancient house!—and all in one afternoon.

We happened to possess a pair of bellows, very old,
of rosewood and red leather and little brass nails: a
smallish bellows, but of such desirable workmanship and
such curves that we had fallen in love with it even though
it lacked a nose, for the enthusiastic collector comes to
disregard a little want such as that; he realises that
everything comes to the collector who waits—or at least
to the collector who looks while he is waiting.

And so it came about that in Amsterdam, walking
together between those charming streets that are half
canal, or canals that are half street, the Keizersgracht
and the Heerengracht, we noticed, in the basement of
a dodderingly ancient house, a tiny little shop; and we
looked at each other with the same gleam of hope, for
it was the shop of a bellows maker; a maker of small
bellows for family use, for the blowing of the charcoal
and peat fires so much used in Dutch cooking.

We stepped down three or four steps into the shop,
and there was a stooping, dark and ancient man quietly
at work at a tiny forge and bench, and we told him that
we wanted a brass nose for a bellows.   But he was un-
equivocally Dutch, and, different from most Dutch-
men, knew not a word of German or French or English,
nor could he understand our signs; and for our own
part we had not a word of Dutch.   He stood and

waited, with his arms rolled in his leather apron and his eyes following us with intelligent alertness. Time was passing, and we were not any nearer making him understand. But still we persevered, and suddenly his face brightened, and he drew open a drawer in an old chest of drawers, and it was full of brass bellows noses, and we chose one, that later was found to be a precise fit; thus giving our old bellows good looks and usability, and adding to its claim of age an association in one feature (its nose) with Amsterdam.

And the chest of drawers!—it was an unexpected treasure, for it was of that much-to-be-desired kind made with three square-edged or curve-edged vertical surfaces, slightly projective from the plane of the front. It was, indeed, a veritable block-front! But it was quite dilapidated; rather too much so, in fact, to justify having it crated and shipped to America; and, anyhow, we were to travel farther, and were short of time that day; and we reluctantly decided upon renunciation, and left the old man, who stood at his door, blinking after us in the sunshine. But as we knew the chest of drawers would be valued by any near-by collector, we told of it to a Dutch friend, who eagerly possessed himself of it for the equivalent of seven American dollars.

A little later in the same afternoon, we were visiting this friend, a retired Dutch army officer, at his home in a delightful Amsterdam suburb; a home filled with rare and valuable antiques, many of them inherited, his father having been a noted collector. But although the suburb and its houses were new, and the home of our friend and his wife—a delightful Dutch lady who speaks perfect English and quotes American poetry!—was new, its front gave a distinct impression of age, for its façade, of ancient style, was topped with a pair of great stone dolphins, of familiar old Dutch type, with tails making the finial at the top.

"And that is really an ancient gable," said the major; "I got it from an old house in Amsterdam that was being torn down. I can be on the lookout for such a front for you, and can get it for you, if you but say the word. You have told me of a block-front bureau in my own city; I will get a house-front for you!"

We could not accept the offer, for such a fishy finial would not fittingly finish the Colonial gable of our home, but the matter-of-course possibility of it was impressively illustrative of what it is possible to find and acquire.

There are some few things that, although modern in make, are essentially antique in character and feeling and assimilate perfectly with the actual antique. For to all intents and purposes they are antique. We mean things that are still made, precisely as they were made decades or even centuries ago, by the descendants of the old-time makers, living in the same localities, making thus a survival of the ways and customs and handicrafts of the past.

Those who are found associated with vanishing industries of the past seem always to be old; like the women of New England who make braided rugs or the ancient dip candles, or the man who makes rush seats just as his great grandfather did, or the bellows-maker of Amsterdam.

The little black shop and the dark old stooping man —that is the kind of place and person associated in some degree with the finds of every enthusiastic collector. And the possibility of finding such a shop and such a man, in this or that or the other place, points out how very much of romance there still is in the world, even in this twentieth century; how much of romance may be found in the path of the collector; for as to collecting, the fine old words are applicable, that her ways are ways of pleasantness and all her paths are peace.

The effect of surprise and romance is so vividly realised by those who would prey upon the credulity of incautious collectors, that the dark out-of-the-way shop, and the dark and stooping man, so located as to be come upon by accident, are sometimes used as a means of disposing of the ten-dollar antique for one hundred, or the false "Old Master" for thousands, "at a bargain." But usually the dark man, in his tiny dark shop, is without guile.

In Florence, one day, one of us happened into the little sombre shop of an old man, on a narrow, back

street. He was a locksmith, and worked as his forefathers had worked. He made keys and mended locks,
and had nothing for sale, but upon a hook on the wall
was a lion's head, of iron, through whose mouth water
had somewhere, some time, gushed.

"Oh, that came out of an old palazzo garden," he
said; which sounded more important than it necessarily
was, for we knew that all palazzo gardens are not palatial.

"*Quanto?*" he was asked.

Whereupon the old man took it in his hands and
turned it over; then, with a look of firmness he replied:
"One lira—" and seemed surprised at not receiving a
lower offer. He wanted the equivalent of twenty
American cents, and was pleased that the American
did not insist on getting it for eighteen! It was a heavy
thing for its size, to take home, and had a way of shifting from end to end of any piece of baggage in which
it was packed, but it is now upon the wall of a little
secluded garden behind our home, and water has been
piped to it, and gushes through the lion's mouth just
as it used to gush forth long, long ago in Italy. And
it is not only an effective thing in itself, but has also
the appeal that comes from association with one of the
most interesting of all the cities of the world.

It was in Florence, too, that enough old scarlet bro-
cade was picked up, from a peripatetic vendor with a
sort of flat barrow, in the Mercato Vecchio, where Boc-

caccio often walked, to bind a volume of the Decameron; thus giving the book of the Florentine an old Florentine binding.

We know from our own experiences and that of our friends, that one is not compelled to go far away from home to find treasures; that fine old things may be found near home; but almost all collectors do, at times, like non-collectors, go away, and when they do there is every reason why they should have it in mind to add to their things of value. If they don't go to Boston they can at least go to their county seat. They may go to Paris, across the sea, or to Paris, Kentucky. Summer vacations often give splendid chances. Business trips may result in valuable finds without in the least interfering with business. A delightful little pair of brass andirons, andirons for a bedroom fireplace, was picked up unexpectedly in the capital of Florida—a State not in the least suggestive of fireplaces—because the owner was tired of the trouble of cleaning them. We all go somewhere; then why not get something when we go there!

A town full of picturesque memories is old Bethlehem, on the Lehigh, associated as it is with the Moravians, with the early settlement of Ohio, with the romance and tragedy of early days, with the Revolution; the old building still stands where Washington visited Lafayette, and the people are still proud of the banner given to Pulaski by the Moravian girls—the "nuns" of

Bethlehem, with "altars and censers," as the youthful Longfellow mistakenly sang.

Any piece of old furniture from Bethlehem would naturally be prized much beyond its intrinsic value, but we were there but a day, and in that time chanced to find nothing; though we took away something as precious as old furniture—the memory of the trombone playing, before daylight on Easter morning, through the town and from the tower of the old church; a custom that has come down through many generations.

No; we secured no old furniture in Bethlehem; but a year or two afterwards, at the home of a friend a hundred miles away, we were told of a corner-cupboard that could be secured for five dollars, which a family, old Bethlehemites, had brought with them and now, on moving away, wished to sell.

So we possess this corner-cupboard from ancient Bethlehem, bearing with it the charming association with so picturesque a town; a cupboard capacious, shapely, dignified, old, and extremely utilitarian.

It is simply amazing that this kind of cupboard has gone so completely out of modern fashion; that modern makers do not make them; for, standing cornerwise, they occupy no usable space, no matter how small the room may be; they are never bumped against for they are so withdrawn; they are firm and reliable instead of threatening to topple like so many a cupboard of pres-

THE EXCELLENT OLD CORNER-CUPBOARD FROM A TOWN OF INTERESTING HISTORY, BETHLE-HEM, PENNSYLVANIA.

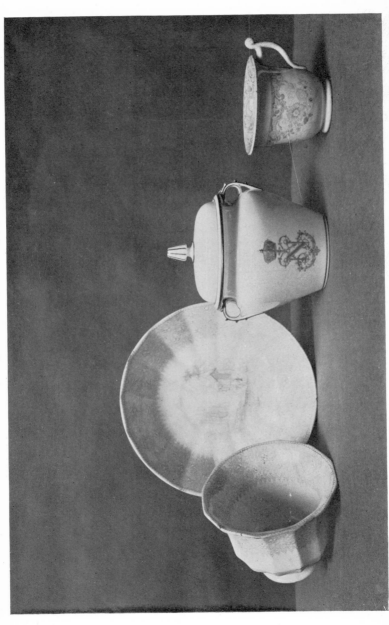

THE CUP AT THE LEFT (STAFFORDSHIRE) WAS OWNED BY MAJOR TALLMADGE; THAT AT THE RIGHT, ALSO STAFFORDSHIRE, BY MAJOR BUTTRICK; THE SUGARBOWL IS OF SEVRES AND WAS MADE FOR THE TUILLERIES.

ent-day make. And good old corner-cupboards may still be bought, in country towns, for from five to fifteen dollars each.

Some time after getting the Bethlehem cupboard, we secured an old chair, a capable, comfortable Windsor, in a little Pennsylvania town; and, burned into the wood, on the under side of the seat, is the name of the maker, followed by the fascinating name of Bethlehem. The collector should never despair!

In the Bethlehem corner-cupboard, among antiques with age but not definite associations, are some whose associations are distinguished; as a cup and saucer, of blue Staffordshire, belonging to the quick-witted Major Tallmadge of Connecticut, to whom, in defiance of the opinions of his immediate superior, and without fear of even the then honoured General Benedict Arnold, it was entirely owing that André was not permitted to escape. These were a gift to us, out of a set, from his grandson. Next them stands a little custard cup that belonged to Major Buttrick, who was the leader of the embattled farmers who stood at Concord Bridge and at whose command was fired the shot heard round the world. There is a positive thrill in the possession of cups that belonged to those brave New England majors, and they put us in veritable touch with the brave days of the Revolution.

In the corner-cupboard also stands a sugarbowl, of Sèvres, whose exquisite beauty and fineness of ware would be notable even without the imperial "N"; and this sugarbowl—we have it on the personal authority of the curator at Sèvres, to whom we showed it and who vouched for its authenticity—was part of a set made for the palace of the Tuileries, and must have been among the loot carried off, during the burning of the Tuileries, caused by the disorders of the Commune.

In ancient Rome there is a rag fair at which, so prosaic folk would have you believe, there is never anything of value. And it is true enough that most of the things offered are valueless to a collector, they being ragged remains and second-hand debris, with numberless jingling modern Roman lamps which would fain be passed off as *"antichita"*—"anti-cheata," as we heard a not-to-be-deceived American pronounce it—and seven-branched candlesticks (to burn!) of spelter masquerading as brass, and terra-cotta figures made a few weeks ago, but broken and bearing the marks of excavation—for they have been in the earth for a few days!

But as it is a legitimate place for things that are shabby there may usually be found there something that is both shabby and worth while; and we bought for a few pennies—and this is mentioned to show, were there no other proof, that it was not something deliberately made to sell as old—a candlestick of Sheffield plate, with the plating somewhat worn but not particularly so. It was past its original condition or it would not have been there; a candlestick fine and dignified, with shaft classically fluted; an Ionic column; thus peculiarly befitting a market in classic Rome.

Few places are so rich in interest as the famous Eastern Shore of Maryland, and in spite of the many years of inroads by collectors, antique treasure is still to be found there. We have obtained some admirable things very cheaply in that region; but it must not be thought that everything antique is a matter of cheapness. There are times when a collector must be ready to pay liberally if he wishes to secure a prize. Collecting is by no means altogether a matter of half a lira or four or five dollars.

A highboy, obtained only three years ago from the Eastern Shore, is a really splendid example of style and workmanship—highboys being those towering pieces of furniture whose lower drawers are set well above the floor by slender, and usually curving, cabriole legs, thus differing from the chest-on-chest, whose drawers come down to within a few inches of the floor. Highboys rise, drawer above drawer, toward the ceiling, and end either in a straight cornice, or in the double curve known as "broken arch" or "bonnet top."

This is a "bonnet-top" piece; it is, in all, eight feet four inches in height and three feet eight inches wide, and its shell-topped, claw-and-ball legs are eighteen inches high. Hawthorne, who liked highboys, says that there is "nothing better than these pieces, standing on four slender legs, and sending a tower of mahogany to the ceiling"; only this particular piece is of walnut, which was greatly used for fine work in early days throughout Maryland, Pennsylvania, and Virginia.

That one of our finds in a famous place was in the home of the American Lord Stirling, is remindful of a find in the ancient Scottish Stirling, the town, rich in literary and historical associations, that has stood for centuries under the shadow of rock-perched Stirling Castle.

For in Stirling we found an excellent example of what is often called early Chippendale, it being in fact a style that just preceded Chippendale and upon which he based much of his best work. It is a heavy chair, of about the year 1730, made of some kind of nut wood; a chair extremely interesting in itself and with the added interest and importance of having been found in so famous a place.

But always it should be remembered that it is not necessary to go abroad to get things from famous places. More and more Americans do go abroad, and therefore have the chance to get things there, but there are also fascinating historical places at home in which it is a delight to find antique treasure.

There are splendid old stories about some of our American towns, such as Deerfield and Hadley. Take old Hadley, for example. They still point out, there, the precise spot where stood the little old church where the people were at worship when the Indians one Sun-

day morning stormed into the town, and they still tell
the brave old story of how the men formed and fought,
and of how it was a losing fight until a gaunt grey man
suddenly appeared, as if by magic, and, rallying the
villagers, led them to victory—and then vanished—and
of how it was the regicide Whalley who, pursued with
fierce malevolence by Charles the Second and hunted
from place to place with a heavy price upon his head,
had been in hiding in one of the village houses till the
call to battle took him unhesitatingly out to save the
town.   The blood fairly tingles at such a good old American tale.

Hadley is a delightful old place, a place of spacious-
ness, with its great, open, elm-shaded green sweeping
and stretching down between the ancient houses with
their dormer roofs and spacious garrets.

And in the garret of the oldest of the houses, uncared
for, stored in a corner, we found two fine old black
chairs, with straight backs of the prized shape known
as banister.   The old couple who owned the house were
glad to sell the chairs and we were glad to buy; and
they are the oldest chairs in our possession, having been
made fully two hundred years ago.

But they are more than old; they are from Hadley;
and they give in high degree the delight that goes with
any veritable old possession from a town of such
stirring and honourable fame.

As we write this, we sit in front of a fireplace whose

fireback veritably came from a royal French château; the old brass andirons were obtained, and very strangely obtained, one summer's day on Blennerhasset Island; the wood is lifted with a pair of tongs used by Aaron Burr in his age and poverty; and the handle of the long iron poker has welded upon its end a grape shot, an inch and a quarter in diameter, fired from one of Lord Percy's guns on the day of the Concord fight, and given to us by a farmer who had dug it out of the chimney of his great-grandfather's house.

CHAPTER VI

THE CHARM OF COMPARATIVE CHEAPNESS

THERE are two misapprehensions that are extremely common; one is, that old furniture is uncomfortable, and the other is that it is dear; although, as a matter of fact, it is quite as comfortable, on the average, as furniture of to-day, and at the same time is distinctly cheaper.

But such terms as comfortable and cheap are necessarily relative, depending as they must upon different standards and upon viewpoints variant. And this matter of different standards is often interesting in regard to other matters, as well as old furniture; for example, the Quakers used to call the home of President Washington, in New York City, a palace, whereas the French Minister referred to it as an humble dwelling—and each was right and each wrong, dependent upon what made the standard.

But by any fair comparison, most old furniture is as comfortable as new, and most of it is cheap compared with new. Old furniture is worth more and costs less!

There are a few Puritanical slat-backs that are as straight and uncompromising as blue laws; but that a very small proportion of old-time chairs are uncomfortable is no reflection on the old chairs that are comfortable. There are also uncomfortable modern chairs—and the memory of certain collapsible backs offered to an audience at a recent lecture comes as a memory of torture.

And yet, after all, one's desire for comfort, one's habits and judgment and ideas as to comfort, may be directed and controlled. It is well to remember that Hawthorne wrote "The Scarlet Letter" at a high and narrow standing desk, and found it easy. Monks have been credited with seeking comfort—yet how straight-backed is the typical monk's bench! It is all a matter of habit and custom.

Many an American demands a rocking chair for comfort; yet one need not look upon even rocking chairs as a primal necessity, for they came in only at the time of the Revolution, and, before that, the generations easily found physical comfort without them. And we know a dear old lady who, loving her rocker, as a chair to sit in, yet did not want it to rock, and had the rockers shortened and knobbed into static position. There are times when nothing but a great fireside chair will give comfort; there are other times when a rigid, rush-bottomed chair is precisely what one desires. There are some who find comfort in lounging-chairs which are absolute misery for people who have from childhood been accustomed to sit up straight. And it is seldom that a chair which a man considers exceptionally comfortable is comfortable for a woman.

There was anciently a time when people reclined upon couches when they ate; yet nobody nowadays thinks straight-back chairs uncomfortable when dining.

No lover of the old thinks that he is martyred by using old-time furniture; there are stiff chairs and easy chairs, dining chairs and resting chairs, there are old-fashioned sofas, comfortable and big. It is possible that the entirely erroneous notion as to old-time furniture being uncomfortable arose from the memory of the slippery chairs of, say, 1860, which was not a period of beauty or attractiveness.

And as to the cost of antique furniture;—one so frequently hears the remark: "Oh, I should love to have old furniture; nothing would please me more; but I cannot afford it!" And this kind of statement, made and repeated over and over again, has had such influence upon the general mind that there has come to be a widespread impression that the collector must be a person of wealth, or at least a person with a great deal of money to spare. Even some who collect, and who really know better—so strong being the influence of any widespread belief upon people's minds—think that collecting is an expensive matter. Whereas, as a matter of fact, it is actually cheaper to furnish one's home with the fine and charming things of the past than it is to furnish with the comparatively unattractive furniture of to-day.

The mistaken feeling has largely come through a confusion of ideas in regard to collecting. The man who sets himself to gather along such lines as cameos, postage stamps, coins, first editions, engravings, etchings, old silver, Old Masters—the man who sets himself to gather expensive extras—must be prepared to lay out considerable sums in addition to his ordinary expenses; for such a man, collecting is an expensive recreation; and if collecting were nothing but that the popular belief as to its being costly would be quite justified.

But throughout, we have in mind collecting of a very different order; collecting of the kind followed by almost all real lovers of old-time designs and workmanship, old-time association and charm, in articles intended for the furnishing and adorning of one's home. The best kind of collecting is gathering definitely for this purpose; it is not gathering as if for a museum. And a house may be furnished with things of the past far more cheaply than with things of the present. It is a matter of the simplest arithmetic.

Much misapprehension is caused, and much mischief done, by the people who write of prices of antiques without knowing about them; the kind of people who love to say: "Such and such a table is worth two hundred and fifty dollars"—when they ought to know and all real collectors do know that better ones can sometimes be bought for ten, and any day for not over fifty; people with only a lazy city-office knowledge, who love to expatiate on the improbability of getting anything veritable for a reasonable sum. It is largely because there is so much writing of this sort that we tell of some of our own experiences, for they are not unusual but typical, not few and chance but many and common and long-continued and of many different places. We and all our kind of collector can find far more delightful old furniture than we can buy, far more than we could possibly house; not always at extremely low prices, but certainly at reasonable prices and lower than those of the machine-made articles in the modern shops.

The ill-informed generalisations of people who are probably sincere but who have certainly not taken the trouble, except in some very slight degree, to inform themselves by personal experience, discourages beginners on the one hand, and on the other puts false notions of value into the minds of many an owner, who thereupon, although he may wish to sell, refuses to sell reasonably and after a while finds that he has lost his opportunity to sell at all.

The boding cry: No more genuine antiques, except at immense cost! should not scare an active collector into inactivity and despair.

Often, the would-be purchaser of an ancient table is shocked because the owner asks ten or twelve or twenty dollars for it; but the same person would not be in the least shocked were he offered, in an up-to-date furniture shop, tables similar in size and as nearly as possible similar in design, for two or three times the sum.

Although opportunities to get excellent old articles for low prices occur very frequently, we have no desire to lay stress upon the most fortunate prizes, for it is not with the low cost of special antique finds that the prices of new furniture need to be compared.

In a furniture shop or in a china shop, where articles of excellent manufacture of the present day are sold, no one hesitates at paying twenty-five, fifty, a hundred dollars and much larger sums. But in the average antique shop or in an old farmhouse or at a country auction, such sums as twenty-five, fifty and one hundred dollars loom very large indeed. When such prices are asked there is always, except in the fashionable and expensive antique shops, some particular reason.

The point of view may fairly be illustrated by a recent happening. We came upon a beautiful Chippendale armchair, of unusually good workmanship and design, and in thoroughly good condition, although not polished and fresh, for which the owner asked seventy-five dollars: a large part of this price being due to the fact that the chair had been in the personal possession of a very distinguished American.

We did not need the chair, or at least just then did not care to pay seventy-five dollars for a chair; we have acquired a number of Chippendales for prices very much

lower; at the same time, we knew that seventy-five dollars was a moderate price for it, in view of its workmanship and its history, and it is still not at all impossible
that we shall some day get it.

But it chanced that we were well acquainted with a
descendant of the distinguished owner of the chair, this
descendant being a man to whom the spending of seventy-five dollars was a matter of very small moment.   And
we had more than once heard him express regret at not
owning something that had belonged to his ancestor.
So he was told of the chair.

But the thought of seventy-five dollars for an historical Chippendale with family associations, made him
balk.   "That is a big price to pay for an old chair,"
said he almost peevishly; "it's good of you to let me
know—but—"   Yet he was sitting in a new chair which
was frankly impossible in shape, and absolutely without
grace or distinction, which had cost at least fifty dollars,
and he was surrounded by a general furnishing of expensiveness which was quite the modern thing: vague,
half-caste but costly reproductions of good old period
furnishings.   It was clear that he would never even take
the trouble to journey up in the country to look at his
ancestor's chair, though it would be but an easy Satur-
day afternoon run in his car.

It is often really difficult for the owner of a precious
antique to get even a moderate price for it. There
seems to be something in average human nature which

makes people hesitate about buying when they know that the owner wants to sell. The same persons who would eagerly make offers to tempt an unwilling owner to part with his antique, draw off with hemming and hawing when they find an owner anxious to get a little money. There are collectors who would rather give a big price to a dealer in a shop than an ordinarily fair price to an owner, in his own house, where the article has for years been sheltered and cared for.

Recently an old lady, a descendant of General Ashe and Governor Nash—the two men whose distinguished names cognomened Asheville and Nashville—wrote us that she had a Chippendale armchair which she would like us to have; she was compelled to sell it, so she wrote, and therefore thought it would not be exorbitant to ask fifty dollars. The tradition was that it had been brought from England; and it had been handed down from one to another with the words: "It's a fine chair; take care of it." This was the chair she wanted to sell; but, she added, she must first get a release, from a wealthy nephew, of a promise she had years ago made him, to let him have first chance should she be willing to part with it. A few weeks later she wrote, sadly: "He has taken it; but he haggled about the price; and he asked me how the chair was upholstered";—how the chair was upholstered! She knew that no one fit to own a Chippendale troubles himself about the upholstering in which he finds it. Our own best chair came to us with the seat plumped up under a log cabin pattern in patchwork, underneath which were two waistcoats, of a length and capaciousness that befitted the olden days, and underneath these was still another stratum, clearly the original covering of the chair, a stuff of heavy and thready weave and in colour a dark deep red—Chippendale's own fancy for the proper covering of such a chair being red morocco. Not one ancient chair in a thousand has retained upholstering in good enough shape to keep or to restore; the collector expects as a matter of course to reupholster, with barely an exception, except when the chair was first covered with some rare tapestry.

The attitude of hesitation in the face of opportunities, hesitation to pay a reasonable sum for a treasure, is really interesting, and it is typical of the attitude of many. Nor do we merely mean hesitation at paying out sums like fifty or one hundred dollars, for the same kind of pained amazement is just as likely to be noticed when the sum asked for some delightful old bit is only ten dollars, or even less. "Was I badly taken in? I paid seven dollars for those andirons." Taken in! It was beginner's luck, rather, for new ones would have cost twice as much.

The old and the "bargain" are so closely associated in many people's minds that to ask a fair price for an old thing seems an injury. Probably a good share of the explanation is that old furniture or china is "second-hand," and that people expect second-hand things cheap. But this entirely overlooks the consideration that, in the case of rare and beautiful things, age is constantly making them more and more worth while. Every piece of eighteenth century furniture is year by year becoming more valuable.

Any article of furniture which has age, beauty, association with the past, must necessarily be "second-hand," if one wants to look at it in that way. A chair of General Washington or General Wayne, or a table that was actually used by Jefferson or Hamilton, or perhaps some article of furniture possessing only a general association with the past but of real charm and dignity, is in the very nature of things a used piece of furniture; but the mere statement of the proposition ought to show the absurdity, the topsyturviness, of thinking that on account of being used it should be cheaper, that use and age have cheapened it. The collector's very practical philosophy is that it is the more precious for having been preserved during so many years.

A good thing to do, for any one who wishes to begin gathering old-time treasure but hesitates on account of the supposed cost, is to go to a shop where furniture of the present day is sold, of excellent make and quality, and to note prices; and then to consider at what prices veritable old things can be bought. The way in which figures mount in buying new furniture is appalling to any one. One had much better get fine old pieces, vastly better in proportion, design, workmanship, than present-day furniture, and he will save money while achieving beauty.

"One hundred and fifty dollars for a mahogany library desk"; we quote from a furniture advertisement in to-day's paper: but we have a beautiful old mahogany desk, large, generous, in every way convenient, which cost us, including the polishing and putting into perfect condition, just forty-five dollars. We could go out to-morrow and again do as well; with a few months' or weeks' leeway we should confidently expect to do better.

"A Sheraton armchair, thirty dollars"; we again quote from to-day's newspaper; and we know just what the chair will look like, with its highly-glazed shine, and its proportions just so wrong as to make it painful to look at if one knows what real Sheratons really are. That we have a genuine Sheraton armchair which cost, at an auction, thirty-five cents, is an extreme example but one which many a collector can duplicate out of his own experiences; although we cannot, as we can with the desk, set the buying price down as that at which a collector may be confident of getting such a thing.

This same furniture advertisement gives many an illuminative example. China closets of oak, from seventeen dollars to eighty, and of mahogany from thirty-three to one hundred; bureaus ranging as high as one hundred and ninety dollars; toilet tables from twenty-five to one hundred and thirty dollars—and constantly the collector finds himself thinking what gems of beauty he could purchase for a small part of such sums.

One of the advertised items is "a dining suite of mahogany, in ten pieces, including buffet, china-closet, serving table, extension table, five side chairs and an armchair," for the sum, offered as a tempting one, of one thousand dollars.   Well, without criticising these pieces, which would doubtless seem sufficiently attractive to a good many people, we need only say, what every collector knows, that with such a sum as one thousand dollars pieces of infinitely superior grace, proportion, dignity, beauty, could be secured.

It is certainly easier, if that were to be the only consideration, to buy new things out of a furniture ware-room than to go out and find the more attractive old ones—but it is vastly easier to live with the fine old things after you get them!

An old table for one dollar, an old chair for two dollars, a pair of andirons for three dollars, though always delightful, must not be looked upon as representing the real values.   The collector should be ready at any moment to pay liberally for something that he really wants and needs, for it must be realised that the number of pieces possible of attainment is necessarily on the decrease.   We know of that almost unbelievable treasure, six matched Sheraton chairs of mahogany, with the Prince of Wales' feather in the centre of the back; which was a fashionable ornamentation, and a beautiful one, when the Prince of Wales was Regent, in Beau Brummel's "Who is your fat friend?" days.   The chairs are well over a century old, and are still in the family of the man who long ago brought them from England.   They were offered to us for twenty-five dollars a chair; but, as is often the case with collectors—and others!—it was not convenient just then to pay out one hundred and fifty dollars.   But we were so in love with the idea and the chairs, that it was not long before the sum was tendered. Unfortunately, however, by that time the ideas of the owner had changed and he wanted fifty dollars a chair. As a matter of fact, they are worth more than that, but we fear that by the time we are ready to hand over the fifty each, the financial progression will have continued!

Often, the experience of the collector who is not able or willing to lay down the desired price for things of preciousness, but who later is ready to do so, is still worse than this, for he finds it to be a case of Cumæan cumulativeness—not only a higher price for each article but a lessening number!

Old-time furniture, in the very nature of the case, cannot have its existent supply replenished.   Therefore, gather ye old wares while ye may!   Year by year, more or less is worn out, lost, destroyed or placed in permanent collections.   In consequence, although the supply is still very large indeed, it behooves the collector to take advantage of any reasonable chance to get what he really wants.

And get as good things as you can. Get a hundred-dollar table for ten dollars if the chance comes, and enjoy the adventure and the triumph of it; but be ready to pay the hundred if necessary. Ten dollars can be spent on old furniture to better advantage than ten dollars on new furniture; a hundred on old pieces better than a hundred on new; a thousand on old pieces better than a thousand on new. For your own satisfaction get as good as you can; aim at excellence, and then see if you can meet the price. Costly thy antiques as thy purse can buy; rich but not gaudy, for the old furniture oft proclaims the man.

As there are times when economy would be impolitic, so there are other times when it would leave an unpleasant memory: there are times when it is a distinct delight to overpay. And such times come when you find that you can take the long-prized teapot, the cherished chair, the table that has for generations held the family Bible, from some old man or woman who would fain keep the treasure but who feels that it must be sold to obtain some money. One can often buy very cheaply under such circumstances—if one is willing to do a contemptible thing. It is right to buy, for the owner really wants the money; but he or she has preserved the piece for many years; has saved it, in a sense, for your collection; has made it possible for you to possess it, and ought to receive a fair price, bearing some relation to what one could pay to a dealer. Romeo and the apothecary long

A FIVE-LEGGED SHERATON SIDE-TABLE; WITH SERPENTINE FRONT,
ABOUT 1790; AND
EXCELLENT EIGHTEENTH-CENTURY TIP-TABLES, WITH THE SOUGHT-
FOR RIMS AND PARTICULARLY GOOD SNAKE FEET.

A SWELL-FRONT, SPLAY-FOOT CHEST OF DRAWERS, OF HEPPELWHITE
 STYLE; AND
A BOW-FRONT SHERATON CHEST OF DRAWERS, WITH CHARACTERISTIC
 REEDINGS.

ago made the point clear: "My poverty, but not my will, consents," said the apothecary. "I pay thy poverty, and not thy will," responded Romeo, as he handed the man the very liberal sum of forty ducats.

To pick up a bargain for almost nothing from a possessor who is indifferent, who cares nothing about it either for associations or beauty, who would far rather have a modern atrocity, and who, if left in possession of the old furniture or china, would infallibly break it or throw it away or dispose of it for a trifle to the next person who happens along—to pick up a prize under such conditions is a very different matter. There is not only the sense of personal triumph but there is the further satisfaction of rescuing an admirable thing from loss and destruction. But to buy cheap by taking an unkind or unfair advantage, or by high-handed "beating down," would give a bad taste. The distinction between getting things cheap properly and getting things cheap improperly is very plain.

There is a kind of collecting which needs to be mentioned, because it is interesting and important in itself and also because it has something to do with giving the general impression of the high cost of antiques: and that is, the purchases of rare pieces, *pièces de luxe,* by the very wealthy, at immense prices.

Articles of rare and elaborate workmanship and of extravagant materials, furniture superbly ornamented and carved, old tapestry of splendid weave and history,

delicate porcelains, ornaments of silver and of gold—
such things are for the wealthy; and it is a very satisfactory condition that there are wealthy people with the
taste, as well as with the ability, to secure and preserve
them.

The actual literal value of many such things is very
large, and the collector's value, coming from rarity and
age, is whatever in addition may have to be paid. In
such cases, there is really no limit; and when one rich
man is bidding against another for the possession of
some rare and superb article which must be obtained that
moment or never, it is no wonder that prices soar. It
is the same principle that makes Old Masters command
such immense sums as they do: that when there may
never again be a chance to secure such a prize, it is
worth precisely as much as can be got for it. It is this
which gives the public sales in London, even more than
in New York, such interest; for England has many
more treasures of art and elaborate workmanship than
has America, and London has come to be a central
gathering place for costly prizes.

But, it should be added, that the situation is complicated by the efforts of some rich folk to obtain artistic
treasures because of the importance of being able to
pose as connoisseurs; people who really know very little
about such things and who are therefore the mark at
which fraudulent imitations are successfully aimed; people who are led on to pay vastly more than should be

paid for things genuine. This class would actually scorn to obtain antiques at a low price; for them, a thing must be expensive or it is not good.

Whether one collects with a slender or a full pocket-book, whether one spends ten dollars or a thousand dollars at a time, there may always be the assurance that the money can be better spent, from even the most practical standpoint, on old furniture than on the furniture of to-day. But always it should be kept in mind that judgment is necessary—judgment in choosing the furniture, in securing it, and then in arranging it in one's home. There are some collectors whose rooms give the impression that they had obtained the assistance of the excellent Captain Cuttle, who, it will be remembered, in an effort to please poor Florence Dombey, laid out for her delectation two silver teaspoons, a flower-pot, a telescope, his celebrated watch, a pocket-comb and a song-book, "as a small collection of rarities that made a choice appearance."

CHAPTER VII

THE CHARM OF FIREPLACES

IT was a very distinguished and clever Englishman who wrote, just a few years ago, that the principal advantage in owning a coal mine is that it gives a man money enough to buy wood for his fireplace fire. Fortunately, however, with Americans, wood is not at all prohibitive in price; and even if it were very dear indeed it would well be worth the buying and the burning, for nothing so adds a touch of the olden time, so fine and attractive and captivating and alluring and charming a touch of the olden time, as a wood fire blazing on the hearth.

And in most parts of America wood may still be reasonably found, for reasonable burning; not, however, for such orgies of burning as fireplaces used to indulge in, long ago, when they had to furnish the entire heat of the house—as in the time when the minister in the Old Manse, at Concord, was given sixty cords of wood a year by his parishioners.

Immense quantities of wood are wasted in our country. Go anywhere and you will see it rotting in the woods, in the fields, by the roadsides; you will see railroad men burning big piles of discarded ties; you will see huge quantities of wood destroyed merely to get rid of it;—and it might be used so delightfully!   As Henry James once said, ours is a wasteful nation.

If you have a place in the country, it is surprising how much wood you get from merely the trimming of your trees and the cutting away of dead branches. "Some little sticks of thorn or briar make me a fire, close by whose living coal I sit, and glow like it."

Nothing is so beautiful but that there are sure to be some people who do not care for it, and so there are some people who do not care for open wood fires: like the heroine of one of Mrs. Wharton's novels who, making her first acquaintance with the home of one of the old New York families, is so ignorant of real attractiveness as to be disappointed in finding that, instead of a gas log, or a polished grate with electric bulbs behind ruby glass, there was an old-fashioned wood fire, with the burning wood now and then falling forward and scattering ashes over the hearth.

Scarcely any single factor is so important in the giving of homelikeness, home comfort, home feeling, home cheer, home atmosphere, as a flickering, blazing, glowing open fire of blazing wood. People who learn to sit about fireplaces find their health improved, and their minds more at ease; they find more sociability, more friendliness, more genial tolerance, and a lightening and brightening of their lives. The instinct to gather together in front of a blaze is as old as nature and as universal as human nature.

Open fires mean much, or ought to mean much, to all sorts of people, but they mean most of all to lovers of the old, for there is nothing that can give a more delightful old-time atmosphere. For the comfort and beauty of open wood fires, for their own admirable sake and their decorative value as a setting for things of the past, every lover of the old should cherish his fireplaces, if he has them in his home, or if he hasn't any fireplaces he should put them in.

Now, it may be objected that things are not accomplished quite so readily as this would imply, and yet, in the whole field of successful homemaking, as of successful old-furniture gathering—which is itself so vital a feature of homemaking—one must come to understand that the thing wanted must be striven for and that if striven for it is pretty sure to be gained. It should not be belittled, as to difficulties, but neither should it be magnified or allowed to seem impossible. One should approach these problems in the spirit so whimsically expressed by Irving in regard to problems of another nature: "This is an arduous task, and, therefore, we undertake it with confidence."

The passing of the American fireplace was among the most curious of home phenomena. With the advent of stoves, of hot-air furnaces, of steam heaters, the fireplace was disregarded and ignored. Houses that had them, bricked them in. New houses were built without them. For about fifty years the fireplace vanished. There was none so poor to do it reverence.

For a long time the entire charm of all things of the past was overlooked and ignored and forgotten, and so it was only natural that this delightful adjunct of antiques, the fireplace, was also neglected and forgotten —although it does seem somewhat strange that its utilitarian value did not save it.

A few years ago the fireplace began to come into its own again. People began to realise that the mere fact that it did not heat so well as a stove or a cellar heater was no reason why it should not still be used as an aid and addition, and so nowadays house-builders are once more putting it in.

There are some fireplaces that are never used, and such fireplaces are really no fireplaces at all. We all know the kind. Fireplaces cluttered and crowded, without and within, fireplaces almost hidden by an accumulation of vases, photographs, tobacco jars, clock, screen, brass-woodbox (empty), ferns, even widespread fans—with not even a chance to make a fire. And always a cold fireplace points to a coldness of nature, for there is likely to be a cold heart with a hearth left intentionally cold. And what a contrast between a cluttered and disused fireplace and the used fireplace that is furnished with old andirons and poker and tongs and upon whose mantel stands a pair of candlesticks and a clock, or an old piece of porcelain, or something else of the long past time!

It is surprising that the purely decorative possibilities of a fireplace are so often ignored. A blazing fire is a delight to look at. One never forgets Charles Lamb's "clear fire and clean hearth." Peat glowing on a peasant's hearth may make a picture that, painted, may hang proudly in the home of a millionaire whose own hearths are unlit. Even a well-laid fire, ready to kindle, has decorative value. A fireplace, out of use for the hot part of the summer, may be made a beautiful thing by laying within it a few logs of white birch.

We early realised the value of fireplaces in giving atmosphere to old possessions; the more warmly and readily, no doubt, because we lived for a time in an old house whose fireplaces were eighteen; and when we came to live in a house that had only three, our thoughts lightly turned to thoughts of more; and so it is really out of enthusiastic personal experience that we write. And we know of others who have felt similar enthusiastic desires and who have similarly triumphed.

In many an old house the bricked-up fireplace, though it faces you with such an air of finality, may easily be opened. We lived in a house some years ago whose fireplaces had been bricked in for half a century, and we opened two of them in half an hour each. A crowbar, a little energy, a broom—and two fireplaces were made to glow where not one glowed before! Many and

FIREPLACE BUILT INTO A BEDROOM AND GIVEN AN OLD-TIME MANTEL.

FIREPLACE BUILT INTO THE DINING ROOM; OPENED INTO THE BACK OF A CHIMNEY.

many a house has such fireplaces, awaiting such simplicity of treatment; and even in those houses whose fireplaces have been closed and their chimney flues used for the conveyance of furnace pipes the problem is not insurmountable, for the chimney-breast may be widened with wire lathing and the pipes put within that. It is quite safe; it is not as if old-fashioned wooden lathing had to be used. And, then, it only needs the centering of the fireplace opening and a shifting of the mantel-piece. Of course there is some trouble involved in getting the pipes out of the flue and placed newly, but the result is so tremendously worth while! And we ourselves have done chimney-breast widening and shifting and centering, and we know of things that others have accomplished, and so we can speak from things that have actually and readily been done.

If you are building a house, put into it as many fireplaces as you can. There cannot be too many! You will not use all of them all of the time, but you will use all of them some of the time, and you will get into the way of using some particular one pretty much all of the time.

That "MacWhorter would have an open fire" is told in the very first sentence of a recent book by a leading American novelist. But as MacWhorter lived on the top floor of a building in New York City, he was puzzled how to realise his want unless he should build a chimney up through all the rooms from the cellar or else should frankly make his fire in the middle of the floor and knock a hole in the ceiling for the smoke. Whereupon an engineer friend—and the author is himself a distinguished engineer, which makes the story valuable from a practical standpoint—planned and built a spacious chimney-breast, with broad hearth in front, and a chimney rising through the roof above, the whole structure resting upon an iron plate, which was bolted to four upright iron rods, which in turn were bolted to a heavy timber laid flat upon the roof. Clearly we are not alone in believing that you may have a fireplace if you wish one, and the problem is usually far simpler than Mac-Whorter's!

A neighbour of ours completed only a few weeks ago the making of a fireplace in a room that had been without one. It was a new house, not dependent on fireplaces, but built with four or five of them—and one more was needed!

It was on the second floor, and therefore the ceiling below had to be considered. On the first floor it would have been a simpler matter, with only the basement ceiling to think of. There was a chimney in the room, and in it was made an opening for the fireplace, and enough flooring was cut away for the hearth. There being no chimney-breast, and the chimney being shallow, brick jambs were built projectively, so that when all was completed the space for the actual fire was some eight inches in the chimney and nine inches in the room. A broad hearth was also laid. And to support all this new weight two iron bars were built in at an upward angle, from the chimney to the front of the hearth, out of sight, within the floor thickness; and within the floor space there were also half-arched brick. There is absolute safety, and the fireplace looks as if it was built when the house was built.

Although caution should be exercised in placing weight upon a floor not originally planned for it, there should not be overcaution. That a man who would place a heavy piano or a filled bookcase upon a floor, or who would ask fifty guests to gather there, will be frightened by the weight of a fireplace, is a tribute to the baleful reputation of "a bushel of bricks."

Some friends turned their double parlour into a single big room by removing the partition and setting in an I-beam to hold the floor joists of the rooms above. In each room had been an unsatisfactory small fireplace in an unsatisfactory small chimney. So chimneys and fireplaces were removed, and at one end of this new room was built a fine fireplace, opening from an outside chimney built especially for it. The mantel and the tile were white—our friends wanted an all-white effect, and the genuine homemaker always and really wants what he wants when he wants it, and therefore he usually gets it—and in eight years or so the white hearth has not materially blackened; and the total cost of these seeming-elaborate changes was hardly four hundred dollars!

Fireplaces should be neither too small nor too large, but as to this there are no fixed rules. We know of one that has a height, as to mantelpiece, of five feet nine in a room of eight feet six, but it is so successful in these unusual proportions as entirely to justify itself.

It is often supposed that the question of whether fireplaces will draw or smoke is pretty much a question of luck, of mere fortuity, and some have hesitated on that account to have them. A very ancient proverb has it that "if you would enjoy the fire you must put up with the smoke," and the feeling is still widespread among many who forget that the proverb goes back to a time when the methods of getting rid of smoke were haphazard and primitive. But it is nowadays understood that a smokeless fireplace is a matter of proportionate size, and the rule is that the sectional area of the actual fireplace opening should be ten times the sectional area of the flue. If the chimney flue is nine by twelve, a sectional area of 108 square inches, the fireplace opening should be 1,080, which area would best be obtained for good looks and efficiency by making the opening thirty-six inches wide and thirty high. The throat, between fireplace and flue, would in such a chimney be four by twenty-seven. When a three-inch opening can be used it is often still better, as narrow throats tend toward concentration of heat and obviation of down draughts and eddies. But if too small there would be choking and a poor draught.

Very deep fireplaces, built with intent to secure a draught, are a mistake, for they waste fuel and heat, and the depth is needless.

The jambs should run back at such an angle as best to radiate heat into the room; if they run back squarely they throw heat back into the fire itself.

An iron fireback throws out a great deal of heat that would otherwise not reach the room, and at the same time it safeguards the rear wall from crumbling through the intense heat of the flames. And that ancient firebacks, from old houses, are still to be acquired, is one of the delightful features of collecting.

Attractive though fires on the hearth are, it should not be thought that they alone are enough to give old-time charm; suitable mantelpieces are also needed if charm is really to be won. Many and many a fireplace is ruined in appearance by an incongruous mantelpiece, and many a houseful of antiques thus loses its attractiveness. There comes the memory of a house, rich in old furniture and china, whose effectiveness is immensely lessened and whose harmony is quite destroyed through the ugly, tawdry mantelpieces that insistently catch the eye and cheapen everything in the rooms. It simply never occurred to the collector who owns that house that he ought to have replaced the unfitting mantelpieces with some of old and admirable design.

On taking over our present home we found two ugly mantelpieces of oak with jigsaw carvings and little cavities and brackets to put "ornaments" in and on. These were replaced with veritable old-time mantels, taken from a house in course of demolition, and the appearance of the rooms was inexpressibly bettered, and the mantels give no suggestion whatever of interpolation. That they were actually saved from a big bonfire recklessly fed with wreckage from the old house that was being demolished gave an unusually keen sense of satisfaction, of real enjoyment; and, too, the circumstances so reduced the price that the foreman deemed himself much overpaid by a small sum.

Now, the lover of the old cannot count upon discovering an old mantelpiece just as it is about to be consigned to the flames; the point is, that when he wants a mantel he should look about him with the fixed idea of finding one, somehow and somewhere. We never duplicated that particular experience; we did not need to do so; but when we needed another mantelpiece we found it.

This third was discovered at the door of an auction house in Philadelphia. In a few minutes it would have been carried in and set in the warehouse for regular sale and we should never have seen it. As it was, the inquiry was at once made: "Do you sell at private sale?" They did; and two dollars and a half was the price; fifty cents was the cost of shipment by express; and thus for three dollars we secured an admirable old mantel which at once took the place of a modern one of over-ornamented oak. For the actual work involved in taking away an offending and offensive mantel and putting a good one in its place is simplicity itself.

As to putting in fireplaces where there never were fireplaces before, perhaps some of our own experiences may be given, as matter-of-fact encouragement for those who may wonder or hesitate.

The library imperatively demanded a fireplace, but had none; there was but a chimney-breast, sheer and bare except for a stope-pipe hole far up toward the ceiling. That hole was an annoyance to the eye, and so it was filled in and plastered over. And then the mason cut out the space for the fireplace—a work very easily done. The chimney-breast projects two feet and eight inches into the room, thus giving ample depth for a fireplace; more depth, in fact, than is really necessary, but, on the whole, it gives an air of comfort and dignity, and it permits the putting in of big logs.

That the entire chimney was supported upon a stone foundation built up from the cellar floor simplified the situation materially. This foundation was solid, and we let it remain so without attempting an ashpit for the ashes to be dropped through and removed by opening a little iron door in the chimney-base down cellar. A new house or a new chimney can easily have this labour-saving and dirt-saving device built in. At the same time, most fireplaces get along without them.

The space between the fireplace opening and the mantelpiece, above the opening and at its sides, must be covered with some fire-resisting substance—brick is excellent, plain plaster is good—in any case, it should be something very simple. For this particular fireplace, plain, unglazed, bricklike tile, dull-red of hue, are used and the same tile are on the hearth.

Beneath the hearth there is no beam, no wood of any sort. Wood anywhere beneath the hearth, even if safeguarded by cement and asbestos, would be a fire danger. In making this hearth it was necessary to take out a floor joist for the fireplace width, and the ends of the joist were strongly boxed. Then an arch of brick springing from the stone foundation was built, with its outer edge resting against a joist far out and away from the fire heat. The space between the arch and the hearth tile was filled with cement.

The hearth projects twenty inches. It needs to be as large as this for fire safety; indeed, four inches more would be an advantage, especially with a fireplace that has steady use. And for the sake of good looks the hearth should extend precisely as far to the sides as the edges of the mantelpiece. To build the hearth merely as wide as the fireplace opening, as is often done, gives an aspect as of giving the fireplace a little brick apron.

The wall at either side of the fireplace should not be less than eight inches thick, and there should be no lath or other wood within it or directly against it.

The chimney-breast in this room was of mean and boxy size and, through some causeless freak, was not

THE MANTEL FOUND AT THE AUCTION SHOP DOOR.

FIREPLACE IN A BEDROOM. THE SIMPLE MANTELPIECE IS OF THE TIME OF THE REVOLUTION AND COULD EASILY BE COPIED.

precisely in the middle of its wall. As it was, it simply would not do, and so it was widened on one side by a necessary eighteen inches of plastered front, and when the entire room was finished and papered not only was there no indication that the fireplace had been inset, but there was not the slightest sign that the chimney-breast had been altered. Behind the eighteen-inch extension there was a space that was made into a convenient closet for coats and hats.

The second floor of the hall had a fireplace and did not need it, and the bedroom on the other side of the hall needed a fireplace and did not have it. Yet there was no great difficulty about it. It was merely a matter, as to the wall, of bricking up the hall fireplace, taking off the mantelpiece, and papering the wall; and, as to the floor, of taking up the hearth and laying flooring; then, in the bedroom, the back wall of the fireplace was opened flush with the wall, as a new fireplace on the reverse side of the chimney; and mantelpiece and hearth were duly put into their new places.

Fireplaces are particularly delightful possessions for the lover of the old from the fact that their appeal is not only to other old-time enthusiasts but is practically universal. The hearth-fire has stood from time immemorial for what is finest and best in life, and from time immemorial there has been mighty appeal in the *"pro aris et focis"*—the "strike for your altars and your fires." But who would dare demand that you strike for your steam-heater or that you be ready to offer up your life for your hot-air furnace!

Shakespeare, who so often shows what a friendly, kindly, genial, sympathetic man he was, and how he notices and loves the pleasant little things of home, throws out, as if inadvertently, an ever-memorable suggestion of what goes to the making of a home evening: a cosy room, a round table, something of savoury tang, and a blazing fire.

CHAPTER VIII

THE CHARM OF AN ADVANTAGEOUS SETTING

IT is not only fireplaces that are important in the giving of the proper atmosphere to antiques, for there are many possibilities besides, and these possibilities, in the old-time air that they give to the general surroundings, may even approach in significance the antiques themselves. Colours, structure, general character of design—almost an infinity of details—may be used in the effective and natural setting of antiques.

It is not nearly so well to have a great many old things, and merely to crowd one's rooms with them, as it is to have a much smaller number of articles and have them placed in advantageous environment; this needs to be said, for many a collector has kept on packing into his home quantities of expensive antiques, after his rooms are more than full, and has thus altogether failed to win effectiveness such as is secured at houses where the total of antiques may be small and their cost not high, but where there is careful attention to the setting.

If there were anything in the world capable of standing unassisted, it would seem to be Shakespeare's plays, and yet Shakespeare himself, so far from letting his splendid dramatic conceptions stand by themselves, was

keenly desirous of having them surrounded and presented with proper accompaniments. Colours, shapes,
designs—such matters were of vital importance, in his
eyes, in the setting of his plays. Take his Henry the
Eighth: in that play he sets down specifications for even
such details as the pearls to adorn the hair of Anne
Boleyn, and gives directions regarding the mace of the
mayor, the sceptre to be borne by a certain marquis,
rods, robes, circlets of gold without flowers—thus it
goes, showing how to add vividly to the effectiveness of
the lines. And if the plays of Shakespeare were thus
held, by their own author, to depend so greatly upon
accompaniments and setting, there should be no question
about accompaniments and the most advantageous setting for other things—antiques, for example.

Its every detail of advantageous setting is what
makes Albrecht Dürer's house in Nuremberg so vivid
a memory, and the same may be said of the Leibnitz
house in Hanover, the Musée Plantin in Antwerp, the
Château d'Ussé in the Loire country, for in each of
these the old-time furniture is set off, with marvellous
effectiveness, by the proper surroundings and accompaniments. The principle has been admirably studied and
followed in Stenton and in the Oliver Ellsworth house;
to mention just two of the famous American buildings,
cared for by patriotic societies of women, and maintained with close regard to the advantages obtained
through having the rooms and all the surroundings in

A BEAUTIFUL OLD DEEP WIN-
DOW, WITH FLUTED DETAIL;
RESTORED, WITH WHITE
PAINT, AND EXCELLENT AS
ONE OF THE SETTINGS IN A
ROOM OF ANTIQUE FURNI-
TURE.

AN EXAMPLE OF UTILIZING A
DEEP-SET WINDOW JAMB.

A BUILT-IN CUPBOARD, UTILIZING A NEEDLESS DOORWAY; AND
A FIRESIDE CUPBOARD IN AN OLD CHIMNEY-BREAST: GLASS REPLACES
THE ORIGINAL WOOD PANELS.

harmony with the treasures of old times. The most advanced museum curators, as at the Victoria and Albert, and the Metropolitan, are also realising this and are giving up the old idea of a stiff marshalling of a clutter of old things and following, instead, the plan of having a series of alcoves, each one like a separate room, and each with its setting carefully planned.

The colours in a room furnished with old-time furniture are of vital importance. Colour can help or hinder. In a general way it may be said that a room furnished with eighteenth century things should have its walls of one single colour—that is, not with broken pattern or a variety of colours. The best of all backgrounds is afforded by panelling in white or in light grey, or if this is too difficult, panelling to three feet from the floor, with colour above to meet a white cornice.

If the walls are to be papered there are possibilities in greys and in greens and in yellows; and the yellow might even be as strong as a King's yellow, or pumpkin yellow as it is sometimes more irreverently called! Our own library is covered in King's yellow, above the line of the bookshelves and white panelling, and even from the first we liked it, but like it still more now that it has somewhat sobered and toned. The important thing is to have a plain and unbroken surface of colour; or if some slight design seems really desirable in some particular room, it keeps the best effect to have a plain and simple stripe. In this way, there is opportunity for the eye to see what the contents of a room are like, without the confusion and distraction offered by complicated wall patterns.

If we tell of some of our own rooms it is not because we think them perfect, but only that they illustrate efforts toward proper accompaniments, if only in degree successful. For the walls of one room we chose an English paper, an Adam design, which strongly appealed to us, a paper which we liked very much and still like; it is all white, with an unobtrusive pattern in faint pewter colour, but we now know that the walls would be still better without the pattern.

Perhaps the one exception to broken colour on walls can be made in favour of an old-fashioned landscape paper in a large hallway; reminiscent, these landscape papers, of old halls in old houses in Salem and Portsmouth. These huge landscapes necessitate a wainscot panelling of three feet or so in height, a well-made wooden cornice, no pictures (other than those of the wall print), no gas or electric sidelights breaking through; and then, when the hall is large enough, the greys and soft greens of the stone-pines and classic templed isles of the old-fashioned designs are an ideal accompaniment of the antique.

Chintz-like wallpaper often tempts, for old-time effects and surroundings, but in the end the owner will regret it and wish that the chintz paper were plain.

But flowery chintzes for the windows, chintz on chairs and around the top of a four-poster, are a very different matter, and aid materially as effective accompaniments of the old. The rememberable and suggestive phrase of the delightful Pepys, "Bought my wife a chint," often comes back to us.

Whatever the colour of the walls, the best wood-finish for a house of American antiques is beyond question white, with doors of mahogany: real mahogany, if possible, but at any rate mahogany finish. Real mahogany doors went naturally and effectively with the houses built in the days when they used what is now called old-fashioned furniture; Thackeray properly gave mahogany doors to the Castlewood mansion in Virginia; and they go with houses with old-fashioned furniture just as naturally to-day. And old mahogany doors are still to be found, at times, and secured, at the tearing down of old houses; we have enough for the downstairs of our house, thus found and obtained, and have had them built in; but if actual old doors are not obtainable, new doors of the most-to-be-desired six-panelled design can at least be used. Doors are difficult to keep in order when white; they are marked and soiled very quickly by the necessary handling and touching. And banister rails even more certainly should not be white, but mahogany. The contrast of mahogany rail and white banister is as attractive as a mahogany door in a white door-frame, but except for doors and rail, the woodwork in white is the only effective setting for antiques of American periods.

Floors and their coverings must be given careful attention, for they are a highly important part of the environment of old tables and chairs. And waxed or at any rate polished floors, with rugs, and especially antique rugs, are far better, in effect, than wall-reaching carpets. Antique Oriental rugs go so beautifully with antique furniture that those who have them may well deem themselves fortunate. But gathering antique rugs is very different from gathering antique furniture: our old garrets and old-time country homes were never filled with antique rugs from the Orient! The only supply has been, necessarily, in shipments from the countries where they were made, and therefore the quantity of rugs that could fairly be called both antique and Oriental has always been limited and is year by year becoming more so. But there are beautiful modern-made rugs of Oriental weave, of not too prohibitive price; and there are Occidental rugs that are acceptable—but though rugs may be Occidental let them never be accidental!

A curious misconception has obtained considerable hold, that rugs and antique furniture clash in period; that rugs do not go properly with old furniture. But a very little study of eighteenth-century paintings and prints and portraits will show many a room with rugs. Over and over, the collector realises the value of old-time contemporaneous pictures as a source of real knowledge of old-time furnishings. And this is a source of knowledge, in galleries and books, that is freely open to everybody, and is very different from difficult deciphering of old-time inventories in remote county courthouses, and old letters and diaries difficult of access.

The basis of this misconception regarding rugs seems to be certain old-time wills and inventories, quoted as referring to "turkey-carpets," with the explanation that turkey-carpets mean table-covers. Well, perhaps some of them were used as table-covers, but at least a great many of the so-called turkey-carpets were rugs. And, in any case, inventories are always apt to be misleading, from differences in usage as to names: a word may easily mean one thing in one country and period and something quite different in another country and period —just as "carpet" means something tacked down, in modern acceptance, whereas the Aubusson "carpets" of old French portraits were rugs, in our modern sense of the word. But there is no mistaking old-time pictures, when you see an eighteenth-century worthy painted as standing upon an actual Oriental rug!

For rooms of lesser importance; for bedrooms, and perhaps for halls; rugs of early American weave or braided rugs are decidedly attractive, if made as the old-time weavers and braiders made them. Mercantile rugs of the present day, turned out by factories in imitation of the handloom rugs of the past, are likely to be failures; to this mercantile imitation of the old there may fittingly be applied the rhyme about the little girl who when she was good was very, very good, but when she was bad she was horrid. It is best, if one can do so—and this is still in many cases possible—to establish a connection with some elderly woman of some inland village, who still makes old-fashioned braided rugs in the old way. But even in such a case it is needful, in sending on the material—for the real rug lover collects the material herself and sends it on to be prepared and braided—to send colours that will work out the desired colour result for the room in which the rug is to be used.

Among accompaniments that aid in making an advantageous setting are doorknobs; and we use the word accompaniments in this sense of making a setting for old-time things, in a somewhat different way from the word accessories, which are themselves old-time things, but the smaller and minor ones. Accessories, as we take the term, are themselves old; accompaniments may be old or new, like rugs, but must aid in the general environment. Doorknobs, therefore, may be either old or new, but the veritable old ones add a charm, with their fine-coloured brass or well-cut glass, that new cannot give, and repay the trouble of adjusting and fitting the spindles and rosettes so that they shall be firm and strong in their new position. No degree of age could ever make a white porcelain doorknob or a mottled one or one of turned oak, worth while!

Our present house, when we took it, had in it scarcely a single doorknob of brass, and it has been a keen pleasure to gather, gradually, enough old brass knobs, and a very few glass ones, to fit the doors throughout every room.   The getting of the knobs has itself been a series of delightful experiences, and each one is remindful of some particular place or happening.   Some are from doors that our forebears opened in their daily round of life, some from friends' old homes, now torn down through city changes, some from a Shaker church, now gone, some found in village carpenter shops, some have been oddly chanced upon, some have been brought in friends' coat pockets, and each one or each pair has its particular history, from the big rare oval, ribbed and rayed, from a door in old Bond street in New York, through various sizes and kinds to the delightful little brass knobs for the doors of a cupboard.

But it must be realised that there are times when a knob or handle needed to complete a door or a piece of furniture fittingly, can be had only in modern make in imitation of the antique design.   For our own part we have found enough of the genuine old, in doorknobs, but it has been through a long course of watching and waiting.

Doorknobs naturally bring to mind door-knockers; and for these, again, there are opportunities for getting genuine old ones.   And, at least, good shapes of modern make and unlacquered finish, so that they can be polished, are to be had.   Although brass knockers and big brass latches are, to a collector, preferable, good old iron knockers are often very well modelled.   For ourselves —merely to suggest possibilities—our knockers are from such distant places as Quebec and London, and one is iron and the other of brass, and the iron one is big and heavy and was on the door of an old house in the shadow of Westminster Abbey and was obtained through the good fortune of passing and noticing it when the house was being torn down and wagons— "waggons" in London—were busily hauling the materials away.

Pictures are of high importance, as accompaniments which add to or detract from the general atmosphere. It is astonishing what opportunities there are, without expenditure of large sums, to obtain old engravings, mezzotints, soft old colour prints, silhouettes, miniatures, old portraits.   Paintings are a kind of house furniture which may be considered without date.   It is a matter of whether they are good in themselves and whether the subject and appearance suit a particular room.

Really old pictures, if they can be obtained, even though of simple kind that one can scarcely hang except in a minor bedroom or the garret—old-fashioned curiosities, hardly to be deemed pictures—or better ones when they can be found, enhance and are enhanced by a setting of things of their own period.   We happen to

AN UPSTAIRS HALL, SHOWING USE OF OLD CHINTZ FOR CURTAINS
AND OF RUGS OF OLD-TIME CHARACTER.

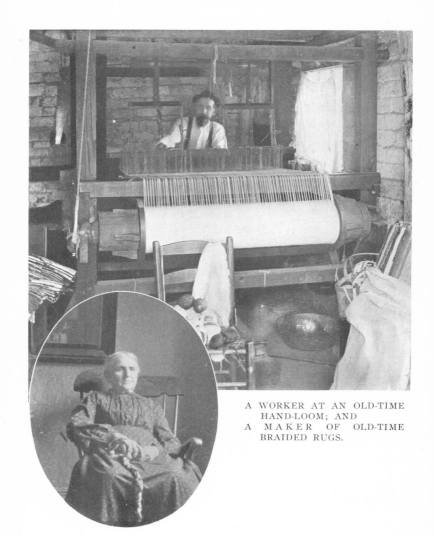

A WORKER AT AN OLD-TIME
HAND-LOOM; AND
A MAKER OF OLD-TIME
BRAIDED RUGS.

be so fortunate as to possess a series of engravings, printed in colour, soft and tawny, over ninety years old, that came by inheritance, and which represent places famous in the career of Napoleon. They hang, each one in a narrow black frame, in the hall, and would be deemed excellent, whether judged by the standards of to-day or of the time when they were made.

But one thing is important, and that is, that no one should permit his home to be injured in effectiveness by unfit pictures, merely because they have come as gifts or by inheritance. This, which is true of any kind of household object, is of peculiar importance in regard to pictures, because pictures, more than anything else, come in one of these two ways. They do not easily wear out, and therefore they are in continuing condition to pass from one to another by descent, and they are a prime object of the gift-maker's intentions. When they are not attractive, they should be banished, put in a portfolio—done away with. And this applies not only to pictures but to every kind of furnishing. Why a person who would not wear an unfit gown or coat or hat, even if it came as a gift or from an ancestor, should be expected to ruin his rooms with ugly or incongruous pictures or rugs or chairs, is incomprehensible. One's house, and every room in the house, become part of oneself, and represent oneself, and should not be at the mercy of the mistakes of well-meaning friends or forefathers. And pictures do certainly offend more than any other class of furnishing. Happy the man whose grandfather's taste lay in mezzotints and old prints!

How one sympathises with one of the orders given to Moses when in the Plains of Moab; for he was directed, as soon as he got into the Land of Canaan, to drive out all the inhabitants and then, before the smashing of idols and the tearing down of high places, to "destroy all their pictures." Well, there are pictures so bad that your whole impulse ought to be for destruction. A famous modern artist, of ultracritical temper, found savage fault with a picture that belonged to a friend. "But it came as a Christmas present," replied the unhappy man. "And aren't there other Christmases to pass it along!" retorted the artist; who was peculiarly a man, however, who would without hesitation put it out of existence, gift or no gift, instead of permitting it to exist.

Yet a well-chosen gift may be the extreme of attractiveness; as, a half dozen bull's-eye panes of glass, taken with great care from the old home of one of our ancestors when it was being destroyed, and thus having the double charm, for us, of association not only with the past but with a family past.

And these six panes fitted at once into a scheme of accompaniments of our home: for we had put in, replacing a narrow outside door of our library, a great door obtained from a house in course of demolition— how very much can be obtained when old houses are destroyed!—a Dutch door, not made in Holland but here, and known as Dutch because it is of the kind that, following an ancient Holland custom, opens in halves, one half above the other; and we needed a broad transom light above this door instead of the narrow light that had fitted above the narrow door, and these six bull's-eyes, coming so opportunely, were set in with leaded frames and precisely filled the space. All collectors know that there are facts like fairy tales!—lids that fit, tables that match, candlesticks that pair; the right thing for the right place at the right time.

As further illustration of the possibilities in accompaniments we may mention a very old bull's-eye from an ancient house, a cottage, overlooking the field of Flodden; a house older than the battle, although this old pane of glass is not itself so old as that. In that battle, four centuries ago, an ancestor of each of us fought —on opposite sides—thus making anything ancient, from an ancient house at the edge of the battlefield, of peculiar interest to both of us. The house was untenanted, but, looking in, the bull's-eye was seen in a window looking out on the garden, and then a visit to the owner's agent resulted in gaining the ancient pane in exchange for a new pane set in by the village glazier. It was broken a little in carrying it home, for ancient panes are not of even surface and bull's-eyes give additional unevenness; but even as it is, it is still large enough to fit as one of the lights over the front door, thus adding distinctly to the old-time look of the house.

Bull's-eyes, which were made of necessity in the centre of each old sheet of glass, were the knobs left where the workman's long tube, his pontil, on which the sheet had been whirled, was detached, leaving a shiny concave lump on one side and a sharp break on the other. Bull's-eyes are picturesque things, but a little dangerous if in the direst sunlight, for they have been known to form burning glasses. They are not made in modern methods of glass manufacture but are imitated for sale, but we have never seen any that have the look of the genuine.

The building in of ancient bull's-eyes, or of old doors, such as the big Dutch door, is but illustrative of possibilities that may come to any one, and we do not mention incidents or possibilities that could come only to ourselves. Old doors may even be obtained, of all places, in New York City! For in charming old Deerfield, that delectable town of fine architecture, of fine old houses, of fine gambrel roofs and fine doorways, the finest door of all was taken from an old house that was being torn down in Grove Street, in that interesting part of New York that is known as Greenwich Village.

It is not only indoor but outdoor accompaniments that may add to the general atmosphere, and of outdoor accompaniments there is nothing more delightful than gardens, and flowers that have definitely descended from flowers that grew in some Revolutionary garden. Surely that would add to the pleasure of any one.

At Mount Vernon, for small sums which are put into the fund for the maintenance of the famous old place, there are sold such things as magnolias grown from a tree planted by Washington himself, in the very year of his death, sago palms from the only greenhouse plant now living that was at Mount Vernon during Washington's lifetime, boxwood grown from garden-bed borders personally planted by the great general and President, Mary Washington roses, profuse blossomers, from a plant which, so the pleasant old tradition has it, was introduced by Washington and named by him for his mother. With such suggestions for a beginning one may go on adding almost illimitably to plants and trees and flowers of association: as hollyhocks from Lower Brandon; Virginia creeper from the summer home of that Mary Phillipse whom Washington wished to marry before he courted a widow but who married an English officer instead; walnut trees from a tree planted by that man of delightfully picturesque name, Charles Carroll of Carrollton, who, when he wrote it thus in full in signing the Declaration, remarked that he did so in order that the British might know precisely which Carroll it was who had signed, though without the explanation it would naturally be thought that he so wrote it from love of the rhythm of the name, as Colonel Carter loved Colonel Carter of Cartersville.

But, outside of definite associations, one's garden ought in itself to be of a kind to go fittingly with old-time things. There are such infinite possibilities of charm in a garden; and there come to mind myriads of gardens and myriad descriptions of gardens. "A garden circummured with brick, whose western side is with a vineyard back'd; and to that vineyard is a planchèd gate—" How Shakespeare did love gardens!

And as we think of old-time gardens beside old-time houses there comes to mind the ghost of a garden facing a stream—a garden facing the splendid sweep of the James. We were going in leisurely fashion up the river, in a little open launch, and were stopping at one beautiful old mansion after another, from Lower Brandon to Westover; and not far from Westover we tied the boat at an old-time landing-place and went up to see an old house famous in early days, famous alike for beauty and for gardens, old Weyanoke. Up through fertile fields and past fig thickets we went, and there stood the house, guarded by two immense strange trees; "cotton trees" they called them, but they were not cottonwoods. The house had been gaunt and desolate for many years, and its grounds uncared for, but just that very year it had been bought by a new owner—fittingly a Virginian to buy this Virginia house—and an air of thrift and gentle care had fallen upon it. The hall was broad, the staircase fine, and the banister formed like Chippendale's Chinese chair-backs. With the daughter of the house we walked out on the side toward the river, and there, near the water, stood two great crèpe myrtles in bloom, marking an old terrace edge, and the girl said: "We did not know that there was a terrace or a garden at Weyanoke, but in the early spring this field was ploughed and all this slope down to the river came into bloom; hundreds and hundreds of bulbs, smothered by weeds and sod, blossomed, and showed us where the acres of garden had been."   Thus between the fine old house and the mighty river rose the ghost of a garden a hundred years old—a setting for the old mansion of Weyanoke, a welcome to its rejuvenators.

CHAPTER IX

THE CHARM OF AN OLD-TIME HOUSE

THERE is positive joy, to a collector, in having his old-time treasures in an old-time house; positive joy in having his antique furniture in a house that is in full harmony with it.

Nor does this in the least mean that he wants to live in a dilapidated house, without proper facilities for heat and light, for a love for the past does not properly mean a love for the deficiencies of the past; modern heating and lighting do not in the least take away from old-time atmosphere; and, as to dilapidation, there is no more reason why a beautiful old house should remain dilapidated than there is that a modern-house should be dilapidated. For are there not painters! Are there not masons! Are there not carpenters!

Many old houses are still to be had; somewhat broken-down, most likely—for if they were not broken-down it would probably be impossible to buy them—but charmingly located and awaiting a charming restoration. Yet this kind of possibility is far from general, as great part of our country is so new that even the oldest houses are new, from this standpoint of a lover of the past.

THE HOUSE
AS ALTERED TO HARMONIZE WITH COLONIAL BELONGINGS

AND BEFORE BEING ALTERED.

CORNICING PUT INTO AN OLD ROOM TO ADD TO THE OLD-TIME EFFECT;
WITH OTHER ADDED OLD-TIME DETAILS, SUCH AS THE BRASS KNOBS.

For collectors in the greater part of our country, it is a matter of building a new home in old-fashioned style or of altering a house to old-fashioned style. There should be no particular difficulty about building a new house with the desired spirit and atmosphere; you merely need to choose the right design and see that the architect doesn't improve it. Beware the imp of improper improvement.

And if you already have a house and it is not of the proper style, it is only a matter of making it the proper style. After all, a house is not like the laws of the Medes and Persians, that could not be changed. A house is but a thing of walls and roof-lines and sundry divisions called rooms, and nothing should be clearer than that divisions and roof-lines and walls ought to be altered if they are not right. You are not master of your own house unless you are master of its form. Washington Irving, home from seeing castles in Spain, and dreaming of a château d'Espagne by the Hudson, completed and altered an old Dutch farmhouse and put a Spanish tower upon it, and made "Sunnyside" a house marked to this day with the charming personality of its owner.

That is a delightful example of possibilities. That the average collector will wish to translate Dutch into Spanish is not likely, but he should feel quite equal to making any kind of radical alteration.

Here in America, what is known as the Colonial style

of house, best studied and appreciated from old houses, rather than from ready-made new ones, seems, on the whole, to go best with old-time American furniture; the Colonial being a style, admirably adapted from the English, which fits alike the rich and the poor, and varies from the gambrel-roofed cottages of New Jersey to the fine broad-dormered wooden homes of New England; from the pent-house roofs and stone walls of Germantown to the carefully bonded, black-headed brick town houses of Philadelphia, the stately mansions of the James, the white-pillared fronts that are especially suggestive of the South—such fronts as moved Van Dyck to say that they "seem to assert that a Greek temple is good enough for the residence of an American."

The actual story of the building of the most beautiful old American homes is fascinating, for the owners were students of architecture and intelligently knew what they wanted. Stenton and Westover and Arlington and Mount Vernon—all are such products, and Monticello is the perfect example. Jefferson visited many an old city and studied the old classic buildings, even going to places as remote as Nîmes, and he came back to America with his mind filled with memories of beauty, and his port-folio filled with actual drawings and measurements, and Monticello was the result. Follow his example:—and if you can't go literally to Nîmes, at least climb the hill to Monticello.

We do not speak lightly or carelessly of altering a house to give it an old-time air, but from some knowledge of what people have actually done and from our own experience. For our own house, though part of it was old, was in general outward aspect extremely unattractive and its rooms were small and undesirable, yet it has been so cleared of excrescences and of ornament, so pillared and painted outside and so completely altered as to rooms and partitions inside, as to make it absolutely different—and all for vastly less than would have been the cost of a building entirely new.

Only two rooms in this house of ours came down unscathed from old-time days, a parlour and a bedroom; and we made even the parlour structurally more in the desired period by a cornice that ought always to have been there, and a cupboard of small-paned glass with rounded beehive top.

The dining-room did not possess a single attractive feature; it was in a wing of about 1880 that had all the faults of that bad period; but it was made into an all-white room, panelled and corniced, and given a white fireplace, thereby securing a proper setting for Heppelwhite sideboard and Sheraton table. Incidentally a partition was taken out to give the room what it also lacked, proportion. And the changing of partitions and putting in of a fireplace was neither difficult nor expensive.

The library likewise showed nothing of desired style;

in fact, there was no library, but two small rooms of equal unattractiveness, in another 1880 end of the house. But by clearing out partitions, putting in a bank of small-paned windows, replacing a meagre door with an old Dutch door, covering the walls with yellow and painting the woodwork white, there was made a room that holds old furniture appropriately.

With enthusiasm, with precise knowledge of what you wish to do, with the desire to plan and the willingness to help, the needful structural changes may be made in almost any interior with an ease that is almost absurd when compared with the general fear of attempting them, and at surprisingly small expense.

Throughout, in house altering and home furnishing, great expenditure is not essential. Getting rid of ugly, unsuitable things is not a process of expense. There is a delectable joy in prying out an ornamented over-mantel and gaining the smooth wall of the chimney-breast—a costless joy, too! It is fitness, balance, propriety, harmony, colour, that make for charm in the setting of the antique, and not one of these qualities is to be exclusively bought by money.

The outside of the house required radical alteration: alteration so radical and extensive that for a while it was perforce postponed; but when it was gone into it proved to be very much less troublesome and expensive than had been anticipated. The house, including wings and centre, was fronted by a long, narrow, unattractive single-storied porch, and the wings, instead of being the things of grace that the word would imply, were of particularly undesirable and even ugly design. Our own preference runs to white pillars, and so the house was given white-pillared, two-storied porticoes. In home-making there should, of course, be modesty; but it should be modesty as to achievement, not modesty of aim. One should aim, and buoyantly, at the highest and best possible—and then, feel proper gratification at the result, if even in degree satisfactory, and humble over the degree of failure.

Among the important possibilities that will aid materially in giving an old-time atmosphere is the making of terraces, or at least porches and porticoes paved with brick—and they are so easily made!

The terrace has become so synonymous with beauty that to use the word brings up a charming vision. Such is the force of accepted phraseology that it is impossible to imagine an ugly terrace. And yet so many are still content to step outdoors upon a wooden-floored porch or portico!

And, in all seriousness, it really does seem as if literature is responsible for this; responsible for the making of terraces, in the popular mind, a creation quite too fine and good for human nature's daily food. Terraces have been given over—yielded without a struggle—to the wealthy, to ancient English houses, to poetry, and to romantic novels, when all of us might have been enjoying them.

Wordsworth's "stately terraces"; Shelley and his "ivy that overgrows the terrace"; Milton's "many a tower and terrace"; Tennyson's "moonlight touching o'er a terrace"; Charlotte Brontë's "I stood, methought, on a terrace," as the beginning of some writing particularly fine; Mrs. Wharton with her people going "out on the terrace" to see the "deep blue purity of the night"— alike the writer of the past and the writer of the present day have put exclusiveness and beauty into the minds of the people in connection with terraces, and these ideas of exclusiveness and beauty have carried concomitantly an impression of costliness. And in consequence most of us have done without terraces, as we have without other frankly expensive and palatial things—but in this particular, needlessly.

The advantages of brick flooring, for porches and terraces, are various. If properly laid, it needs no upkeep. It stands wear and tear. It fits an out-of-doors environment. It looks well. It is permanent and it goes admirably, if properly made, with things of age.

We began with putting brick flooring on a small space. At the side of our house, when we took it, was an old wooden porch, with a long wooden step as its approach. From the first it had the usual weak and makeshifty feeling of the usual old wooden porch. And one day, when a friend and the long step crumbled off backward together, it settled the fate of that porch floor. It should be solid; it should be brick. And the change was made so easily!

With an iron-knockered door opening from the porch, and our bull's-eye panes above, and an ancient perforated lantern swinging from the roof with a light in it, that little floor is a fitting accompaniment of things of the olden time.

We were so delighted with the ease and success of this small outdoor experiment that, although not yet ready to undertake an actual terrace, we felt quite equal to the brickpaving of a low-set rear porch, thirty-two feet by ten. A badly rotted floor of yellow pine needed to be taken up and replaced, and we did not see why it could not be replaced with brick; and that there were problems of drainage and foundation made the task only the more interesting. And, too, for any odd jobs of masonry, a man was obtainable who lived only a mile away and who answered one of the many Shakespearean descriptions that show what a homely, practical man the real Shakespeare was, for this man, "was an honest man and a good bricklayer." And that rear porch, brick-paved and with its ancient joint stool and old-fashioned chairs, is another fitting concomitant of the antique.

Following these successes, we could not see why there should not now be a terrace along the entire front. For a little time we hesitated, for we knew and had felt the widespread and ingrained national feeling that terraces could only be for palatial houses. But on analysis there really seemed to be no ground for this. If we could have brick-paved porches we could have a brick-paved terrace. And, as in most cases, so it was with this, that the home-maker only needs to realise clearly what he wants. Where there's the will for a terrace, there's a way. And a terrace is so important a possibility for many a collector's house that perhaps a little detail will not seem amiss.

We remembered the ancient terrace in front of Mt. Vernon, paved with square and smallish slabs of stone, brought from the Isle of Wight. They were so successful in appearance, and appeared to have been so easy to put down, that we felt highly encouraged, especially now that we had had our own porch-floor experiences. And it was not in the least that we aspired to imitation of Washington's home, but only that the details and successes of buildings acknowledged to be distinguished or beautiful have always lessons and encouragement to offer to the homemaker who would himself build with as much success as he can secure.

And, in the outcome, there was no more essential difficulty in brick-paving over one large space than there was over the several smaller spaces.

There was a bordering layer of bricks laid on edge, on a stone retaining-wall eighteen inches wide; below grade, this was of rubble-work, and above grade broken-joint

TERRACE ADDED TO THE OLD-TIME HOUSE; WITH ADJUNCTS OF OLD SETTEES AND OLD WINDSORS.

STENTON, A CHARMING EXAMPLE OF OLD-TIME ARCHITECTURE; FULL OF IDEAS FOR THE BUILDER OF TODAY.

work. To inclose a larger area details had to be more carefully seen to than with the little porch floor with which we began, and the stones were laid on their flat beds, with a through header for every ten square feet of wall. The stones were laid in lime mortar, made of fresh-burned lime and clear, sharp bar sand, heavily gauged with cement, and all joints above ground were carefully cleaned and pointed with Portland cement.

The large inclosed space was filled with earth, largely obtained from the foundation-wall excavation, up to within eight inches below where the brick were to go; and this earth was over and over again puddled and tamped to settle it, and then a week of heavy rain came in opportune aid. Above this earth was put eight inches of cinders, thoroughly tamped and rammed; and then the brick were set in a layer of sand. The brick were laid flat, in thirteen-inch squares, with a half-brick in each centre.

There were two cellar windows, at the front, to be cared for. We could have done like an acquaintance who, in building a big wooden porch at the front of his house, shut up the cellar windows, leaving that part of the cellar in unsanitary, unhygienic darkness; but it seemed better to leave two rectangular areas in the pavement, to conserve the light. These are shut in with set bars, fixed in cement, and are thus strong when stepped upon and, incidentally, burglar-proof.

With this long open terrace, which was most of it to be open to rain as well as to receive a good deal of drip from the eaves, there was the matter of drainage to be seen to; and so, not only were the bricks laid at a slight slope, invisible to the eye (a precaution, this of the slope, that should not be neglected even with a small area), but a drain was carried from the bottom of each cellar-window rectangle, out under the terrace. These drains, laid before the terrace was filled in, also carry the water from the down-pipes at the front of the house.

And the terrace is in front of our white-pillared, green-shuttered, dormer-windowed house, and upon the bricks stand two ancient settees and several Windsor chairs; and it seems to us that every collector who is also a home-maker—and every collector ought to be a home-maker—should aim at a terrace as an accompaniment to his antiques!

Collecting, it will be seen, properly involves very much more than merely the getting of old-time furniture; it of course involves that, but at the same time ought to involve so very, very much in addition; you may hitch your collecting chariot to a star or to a glow-worm—there are times when one seems as bright as the other—but there will be immense difference as to where you get with it!

There are so many things that can be done, so much beauty about the fine old buildings of the past to emulate!—and as we write this there comes to mind a myriad of things that a lover of the past could well copy; as, to mention only a single thing, the semicircular stone steps at Westover, rising from the box-bordered path by diminishing semicircles to the great door with its broken-arched pediment.

And the panelling of those old houses and the thousands of other old houses—how remindful it is that panelling ought never to have gone out, that it should never have yielded to wall paper, except for minor and unimportant rooms. But even panelling, with its fine air of association with a fine past, may be put into many a room for which it was not originally planned; we have put it into two rooms of our own, and shall some day put it into one or two more; and it should be added that panelling may be expensive or it may be comparatively cheap, only it should not for a moment be forgotten that cheapness should never be permitted to be lack of proportion or lack of design, and, even more important, that cheapness should never be pretentious. Its safety is simplicity.

Another thing which, like panelling, went out of fashion but is now coming into its own again, is cornicing, and, like panelling, cornicing serves admirably as an accompaniment to the old. A panelled and corniced room, with Chippendale and Heppelwhite furniture, is far more beautiful than the same room would be, even with the same beautiful furniture, without cornice and panels. And it is even more easy to put a cornice into an uncorniced room than panelling into an unpanelled room.

We find ourselves constantly illustrating with our own experiences because it is through our own experiences that we have practically learned that there is so much that can be done. Our own experiences, therefore, are given, as encouragement to show that if we can do such things with collecting and home-making, anybody may confidently expect to do such things: anybody, that is, who is willing to take collecting and home-making seriously and to understand that collecting of the proper sort means not merely the gathering of curiosities but the using of them in the making of a home.

Fascinating possibilities present themselves in endless succession. One early realises that cupboards of Colonial design are a beautiful thing in which to keep old china; that there are two kinds of cupboards, the movable and the stationary; and that the movable can still be picked up, in many and many a place, although not always for such a nominal sum as the five dollars that was all that was asked for our corner-cupboard from Bethlehem; and then one ought to learn that stationary cupboards may be built in your house if your house does not possess them.

Old china perched precariously on hanging-shelves or other things shakable is never safe. It should never be housed hazardously on tables. Even the old corner cupboards have not quite the solidity and advantages of a cupboard impossible to move. Constantly one comes back to the realisation of the perfect safety of china in a solid built-in cupboard.

In one of his delightful essays Charles Lamb tells of his love for old china being so great that, when he goes a-visiting, his first inquiry is for the china cupboard—or china closet, as he calls it, thus implying that the china was out of sight behind wooden doors. And when it came to us that we should ourselves build in a permanent and much-needed cupboard, this out-of-sight feature we wished to avoid. It seemed desirable to have old china in sight; with reserve, of course, but still so to show itself that no stranger would need to make Lamb-like inquiry as to its location.

We wanted the new cupboard, on account of its contents, to be in the old-fashioned parlour of the house, for we had frequently felt the charm, in houses in England and Holland, of the drawing-room cupboard, filled with old china.

At first sight, the parlour offered no place for a cupboard. It is a room with somewhat less than the average amount of wall space, because of having windows on the north side as well as on the south. Yet none the less we wanted a cupboard there. One corner seemed to offer the only possibility, but even this corner was a solid bit of wall, looking very permanent, with a picture on it and the tip tea-table sedately in front. Clearly, something else must be thought of.

After all, what the home-maker needs is practical imagination, and practical imagination is a pretty general potential asset. Any of us should possess it; it is nothing essentially extraordinary. One of the greatest encouragements to the ambitious home-maker lies, rightly considered, in Shakespeare's delineation of the homely Quince and Bottom, Snug and Flute, for these extremely ordinary, men (to say the least!) pictured to themselves, at will, a wall present or a wall absent! Well, we saw that all we needed to do in planning for the cupboard was to picture a wall absent!

The possible location was a space four feet wide between the fireplace and the front wall of the room; and the space was recessed two feet from the rectangle of the room. And the natural thing to do was to build the cupboard right there, within the walls, for the cupboard could be deep enough for nine-inch shelves and still leave the proportions of the room unaltered and the recess undestroyed.

We were in possession of a charming old fanlight, picked up a year before in the garret of a famous house in old Annapolis. We always feel an impulse to acquire such a fine old fragment, even though, as in this case, there is nothing but a nebulous idea as to its possible use. Well, here came the use—for it was precisely the thing to top a china cupboard.

The curving line of the top of the fanlight was adjusted to the new position by a rounded casing, cut out of a white-pine board.

There needed to be pilasters down the sides, filling the space between the enclosing walls and the glass doors. The pilasters are each eight and one-half inches wide, and they are grooved to harmonise with other woodwork in the room. Simply contrived capitals stand at their top. Two doors seemed very much more desirable than one, not only on the score of good looks, but because with two doors it is easier to get at the china. The panes of glass are eight by ten inches, the precise size being determined by the lines of the fan-light.

Each of the shelves is exactly behind a crossbar of the sash; and this old-time idea came to us from studying an old corner cupboard to see just what there was about its simple lines that was so attractive. This placing of shelves obviates a superabundance of straight lines, and at the same time has everything on the shelves showing to the best advantage behind unobstructed glass.

The door frames are as slender as possible compatible with sufficient strength—they are two inches wide except at the bottom, where they are eight inches deep. This slenderness is with the object of impeding the view as little as may be. It would be very unsatisfactory to have an expanse of wood down the middle of a china closet. For neatness and firmness, and to render the cupboard more dust-proof, the doors are rabbeted.

The shelves, following an admirable and old design,

are curved in broad scallops, taking away any possible rigidity of aspect and offering graceful places for the various objects.

A keystone was needed as a finish for the centre of the arch, above the fanlight, and for this we used a little carved classic urn, acquired for a few pennies in ancient Hildesheim two or three months before. It is of mahogany, but was painted white like the rest of the woodwork. A bit of wood of actual keystone shape could have been fashioned by the carpenter, but it somehow added, in our eyes, to the general interest of it all, to use a bit of wood acquired in an interesting place in an interesting way, and, on the whole, it increases greatly our pleasure in the possession of this new-made cupboard, that the fanlight comes from Annapolis, the keystone from Hildesheim, the brass door-handles from an old house in Philadelphia, and the shape of the shelves cut quirklike from the design of the long-past cabinetmaker who built the shelves of Stenton.

In all, considering everything, both as to the general aspect of a house and what is inside of it, the home-making collector should aim, in essentials, to emulate the man so delightfully described by Maarten Maartens, who dropped all his worries, picked up what was left of his fortune, recovered what was left of his health, and made just the kind of home he wanted in the neighbourhood he preferred.

CHAPTER X

THE CHARM OF KNOWING RELATIVE IMPORTANCE AND RARITY

WE remember attending a great sale of antique furniture, in New York, years ago, when we were practically beginners in collecting. The room was crowded with people. Article after article was whisked in, as the red curtains parted, and was held high by attendants, turned, bid upon, sold, withdrawn behind the curtains, and another brought out. We were immensely interested in it all. The excitement was keen, the bidding brisk, the sale well managed. The articles were sold in unfinished and unrestored condition. These sales were held in an auction room presided over by a Maryland man, long since dead, named Norman, known in Mr. Moody's delightful collectors' tales as Saxon. He had made his rooms a gathering place for collectors, a place of delight for the cognoscenti, where one collector was sure to see another, and share in the mild excitement of catalogue marking and bidding and, best of all, getting. The old man had a Marylander's eye for a good sideboard and good mahogany, and a keen enjoyment of a little joke and a dislike of dealers, who were never favoured in the matter of bids.

These sales, very well-known in their day, gave a wonderful opportunity to learn how one's fellow-collectors valued antiques, and there were so many people there that the prices were a fair criterion of market value, and the particular sale we are describing was one of the earliest that we went to. There were many women in front who bid on everything; they seemed to possess unlimited pocket-books and although some of them were saying to each other that their homes were already full they were none the less bidding and buying with careless freedom. The discriminating collector buys in competition with the undiscriminating and prices soar accordingly.

Suddenly, a small cabinet was put up; not over two feet high, a sort of miniature wardrobe in shape, with ogee feet, and two doors of dimly tawny colour on whose panels were paintings rather obscure. When these doors opened they disclosed about twenty little drawers, flat, neatly formed, each with a fine little knob.

Now the fluttering women who had been cooing over claw-feet and heavy card tables, seeing so minor a thing as this, took the opportunity to look ahead a bit in the catalogue to see what came within the next page or two.

A quiet, tense sort of bidding set in. The auctioneer stood up from his armchair; the bids were from far back in the room, from some who had not before been heard from, who had sat unmoved through the fall of many an Empire.

The importance of style and rarity was to the fore. The ones who knew were having it out between them. The little cabinet was fine. It was rare. It was perfect. It was unrestored. It was of 1780 or thereabouts. The paintings were such as Angelica Kaufmann made—they seemed fine enough to be really hers. One of the Adam brothers might have designed the cabinet. Distinction, not size, was being sold; the cabinet could be carried home as a package. It sold for a large sum, now forgotten, and no doubt changed hands later in its career for still more, for such things frequently sell very high. Probably not a person in that room would, in a lifetime, have a chance to get a better one or to get one as good for so low a price.

The cabinet was too good to be showy. It was something of rare distinction and unusual importance, but the majority of the buyers did not know this or take much interest in it.

Auctions are schools and museums are schools and good private collections are schools, and very excellent are all these schools, for they enable the beginner to see a great deal of furniture and to come to some understanding of relative importance; something that no one can realise without seeing a great quantity of antique things and noticing how they are presented and valued.

And he will learn the points that make for distinction; he will learn that a rare thing may be interesting, yet neither very usable nor attractive; he will learn that certain articles are held to be admirable specimens of a period, while perhaps other articles, larger and of more pretence, are held to be of lesser value; and he will learn that comparative value is by no means a mere matter of comparative age. And he will learn, of course, more and more of the different styles.

Little need be said here of the great French styles associated successionally with the name of Louis, for even in France furniture of those styles is practically not obtainable except in reproductions expensively made, and the few originals, here and there, are held at immense prices. It is a field not to be entered by the collector who is not wealthy, and one in which the man of wealth is pretty sure to be deceived, for the prices are so huge as most keenly to tempt the makers of the false, and at the same time to lead them to extraordinary efforts to make their productions seem real.

In itself, costliness is not in the least unreasonable in veritable old French furniture, for the originals were made in the days of the old monarchy, with no sparing of expense in workmanship and in princely adornment; and this matter of original cost ought to have a great deal to do with present-day prices of articles of any old period; it is one of the tests of relative importance; it was one of the reasons why the elaborately-made little cabinet with painted pictured doors and such exquisite structure was so eagerly bid for.

From the first, the grand furniture of the grand styles of Louis the Fourteenth, Louis the Fifteenth, Louis the Sixteenth, with sumptuous carving, gilding, ormolu, inlay and painting, was for the classes, not the masses. It was made for royalty and the nobility, for palaces and châteaux, instead of, like the furniture of the great English styles, for all sorts of prosperous people instead of for the wealthy alone.

At no time was there any really great quantity of Quatorze, Quinze or Seize, and as the French Revolution destroyed a great deal of what there was, and much of the rest was worn out and thrown away, it has really left very little for collectors. About the only way to study these periods at first hand is to see their furniture in such collections as that of Wallace, in London; a collection made by an Englishman, in France, at enormous cost; or at the rooms devoted to the three Louis styles in the Louvre—rooms rather remote and obscure in location but which should not be missed.

Not the least of Louis the Fourteenth's claim to greatness was his broad treatment of artists, for to his mind the designation included not only painters and sculptors, but architects, and makers of furniture. He established a Royal Academy, to take in all these classes; and he gave to a number of chosen individuals, to relieve them from sordid cares and make them thus the clearer-minded for artistic work, pensions and apartments. Boulle, for one—variously cognomened by posterity as Buhl or Boule or Bool or Boulle—was made an Academy member and given *un appartement au Louvre,* and his superb work justified the distinction. He worked for royalty and was royally rewarded.

One sees how it was, in France, that the names of the monarchs were attached to styles, and that if a great artist-artisan is remembered, as is Boulle, it is only, after all, as an appanage to a Louis! For the French monarchs impressed their personality; they took themselves and royalty seriously and so the nation took them seriously in turn.

Had the contemporary English sovereigns made themselves similarly of importance, the fame of Chippendale would have been forgotten in a style termed that of George the Second, and Heppelwhite and Sheraton would have been merged, and their personalities submerged, in the designation of George the Third. But the Georges were absentee landlords, eager to get back to their beloved Hanover, scarcely even condescending to learn the language of the country that gave them royalty and never speaking it without a marked accent, so they never impressed themselves as great sovereigns.

Victoria, following the Georges, gave her name to the furniture of her time, and preceding the Georges were the styles, so-called, of Anne and of William and

Mary, as well as that of the Stuarts, now termed Jacobean.

The earliest American furniture is practically not now to be found, and therefore it is distinctly not worth while to say much about it. It was, like the chair of Elder Brewster, preserved in Plymouth, generally heavy and primitive, for the furniture was made in a new country and amid wild and savage surroundings, and even such as was brought over on the early voyages was seldom of fine make.

Yet even the very earliest articles are not actually impossible of acquisition, for we discovered, in a New England garret, a cradle, of panelled oak, that came over in the ship that immediately followed the *Mayflower*. It is still, so far as we know, in a dark corner of that garret; a veritable old piece out of the past; and the owner, an ancient villager, himself a relic of the past, intimated that he was willing to sell.

Books on old furniture are thick with pictures of the Jacobean, William and Mary and Queen Anne furniture, giving the impression that they are as readily obtainable as Sheraton or Empire; but as a matter of fact those early styles have practically vanished. The collector ought to have some knowledge of them, so as to judge properly of the later kinds and they may be studied in museums. Except for historical interest, their vanishing is not of much consequence, because they were, on the whole, not nearly so fine in appearance as the later eighteenth-century furniture by the master English designers.

And the collector should never forget that beauty rather than age alone, is the criterion of comparative excellence in old furniture. For a museum, an important article of the time of William and Mary is more valuable than one of George the Third, but, for one's own delight, to live with and look at, the George the Third piece is likely to be much the more beautiful and desirable.

There is an undoubted charm in the Dutch style, a kind that is frequently termed Queen Anne; but even this is more a charm of quaintness than of beauty, and the charm is so elusive as to be almost always lost in the reproductions that are freely made.

Early American banister-backs, primly attractive chairs of two hundred years ago, are well worth while, and what are known as thousand-leg or gate-leg tables are particularly so. Such tables, made in the seventeenth century and to some extent in the early part of the eighteenth, are a thoroughly good-looking and capable type and are greatly to be desired. They are oval or round, and their thousand legs dwindle in actuality to eight—but never did eight legs have such positively acrobatic capability of swinging and turning and it is no wonder they were cognomened as a thousand.

They have practically disappeared, but still, in out-

THE OLD GATE-LEGGED TABLE FROM VIRGINIA; IT MAKES AN EXCELLENT LIBRARY TABLE.

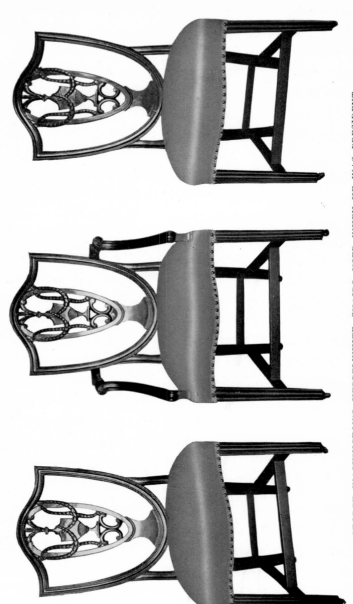

GEORGE WASHINGTON'S HEPPELWHITE CHAIRS, USED WHEN HE WAS PRESIDENT.

of-the-way corners, they may, within possibility, be
found.   Our own is from a little place in Virginia, and
is apparently of not far from the year 1700.   It is delightful to fancy it as being still older, and perhaps it
is—furniture cannot always be dated to a year!—but
there is little satisfaction in seriously dating beyond certainty.

It is of fine, dark walnut, and its top is four feet
five by three feet nine, thus making it of very agreeable proportions for a library table, while it possesses
such a curious outfit of turning gates and hinges in the
top that it will shut into a long, slim, narrow table and
can be quite out of the way when not wanted.

Though oak trees were plentiful, oak never obtained
much vogue on this side of the water, in the making of
furniture, even in the days when England made almost
everything of oak.   The familiar phrase with which
the English pridefully describe themselves, "hearts of
oak," may be taken to refer not only to the hearts in
their own chests but in their chests of drawers.

There is not only differentiation between famous
styles to learn, but a host of little things as well; that
clocks with wooden works are not, as might be expected,
antecedent to clocks with the much more valuable brass
works, but that they came in through enforced national
economy in the lean years following the Revolution;
that rocking chairs were not pre-Revolutionary, yet
that finding rockers on a supposedly pre-Revolutionary

chair does not necessarily make that chair of more recent date, for rockers were not infrequently put upon old chairs; that short pendulums came in later than long pendulums, but not short clocks later than long clocks; that grandfather's clocks, few of which were in America previous to the beginning of the eighteenth century, were not the oldest type of clock, for before them was the wag-at-the-wall, and before that were foot-high clocks with spiral springs and short weights; that if one finds a secretary or chest of drawers or sideboard, with large balls for feet, it must not too hastily be deemed one of the very early and keenly sought-for ball-footed specimens, for those big balls, so rare and precious to collectors, were again used, though not in quite so glorious a size, by the late and decadent Empire, very considerably less than a century ago; and that when a sideboard is seen with feet of these great balls, it should instantly be realised that it is not of the early big-ball period, for sideboards were not designed until about 1770, and thus could not exist with ball-feet of the early kind or even in cabriole-leg designs.

Some splendid armoires have the great wooden balls for feet, and so have some fine old secretaries, and if these are the veritably old they are likely to date back to the very early seventeenth century or at least to very early in the eighteenth. They are very rarely come upon outside of the permanent collections.

A friend of ours was invited, one day, into an old-fashioned house that contained some admirable old furniture, and in a bedroom stood a striking armoire, without feet, and resting right on the floor. But it was of a kind that, as every collector would know, was never made without feet. And so the question was asked: "What became of the big balls that were its feet?" And the owner was amazed. "How ever did you know it had balls?" she asked; and added that they had been taken off years ago, by her grandfather, and that she used to play with them in the garret when a little child. They were at once looked for; and there they still were, under the eaves.

Because there are some kinds of old furniture that it is impossible to obtain except at high cost, a kind of collecting has come into somewhat of vogue that measures by cost alone. There are rich people who buy costly antiques because they really appreciate them but there is another kind of rich people who buy costly things just because they are costly. This latter class have so got into the way of rivalling each other at the great art sales, especially at Christie's and Drouot's, that their buying often goes so far beyond real value as to be comparable only to the buying of Dutch tulips two and a half centuries ago, when fortunes were wildly squandered because all sense of proportion was lost.

Napoleon loved to remark that a throne was only

some boards covered with cloth; yet he well understood the value of a throne and went to considerable trouble to possess one; but he never lost his sense of proportion in regard to it. And even the most beautiful Chippendale, the most sumptuous Louis Quatorze, is but a framework of board, and it is for collectors to decide what it is in addition to that, and to decide without losing their sense of proportionate values.

It is pleasant to realise that the United States Customs department looks with wise discrimination at such antiques as returning travellers bring home, and that the rule as to free entry of old works of art is held to apply to old chairs as well as to Old Masters— to a five dollar purchase as well as to one of five hundred thousand dollars. That is really just as broad and just as wise as the dictum of Louis the Fourteenth that placed furniture-makers among artists. But the rule is very properly applied with discrimination; articles of furniture must be not only old, but art.

After all, discrimination must be the possession of every successful collector; he must gather the discriminate as distinguished from the indiscriminate. You remember Whistler's jibing way of putting it: "You go into a house and find good furniture and apparent good taste. Then you catch sight of something on the mantel that gives the whole thing away." And many a man, touched by that Whistlerian jibe, has looked apprehensively at his mantelpiece!

CHAPTER XI

THE CHARM OF THE THING YOU DIDN'T GET

PROBABLY enough it is true, that it is better to have loved and lost than never to have loved at all; and Fox was probably enough right when he declared that, next to winning, the greatest joy in life is in losing;—and yet the best time to make a collector appreciate the truth of all this is not when some delightful old treasure has just eluded him. But at any rate the charm of the piece itself is sure to be remembered.

We call to mind a really wonderful old chest in a really wonderful old building—the memory of our finding it and thinking we had it and then losing it is very, very vivid; but it was on the whole so interesting an experience that we should be very sorry to have missed it. It was much better to have found and loved and lost such a chest in such a way than never to have found it at all.

We were in Oxford, and were going through one of the wonderful old colleges of that wonderful old town. We had crossed the ancient quadrangle and looked at the timeworn walls of crumbling stone, we had entered the building, and, accompanied by a custodian, had gone through venerable doorways and splendid rooms, and had felt the splendid dignity of it all, the richness of the architecture and the mellowing of time. And in a cloister-like passageway, with groined roof and stone floor, a dusky passageway from which little Gothic doors of oak opened to right and left, suggestive of mystery, we came upon a pile of apparently discarded debris outside one of these doors. There were a few worn-out fur rugs, there was a chair reduced to kindling wood, and there was an old, old chest in a state of shaky collapse—but it was a beautiful chest, beautifully panelled, which would have been noteworthy anywhere and was particularly noteworthy there. "Things thrown away," said the custodian; he was just clearing them out that very day.

We glanced at each other; this was one of those things too good to be true. "If the things are thrown away, I suppose you would have no objection to letting us—"

The custodian was hugely pleased. All at once this rubbish had attained value—not to the college, which had, through some don or proctor or fellow, discarded it, but to him. And he began to drag it toward the door. "You may certainly have the chest," he said.

We were very, very happy. The chest should be strengthened a little, wrapped, and crated, and would stand shipping home. We were very happy thus to secure so splendid and very ancient a chest of oak and such a good ally in handling it, from within one of the oldest and most beautiful buildings in Oxford, and the chest took on a finer charm as it was dragged along through the shadowy passage in a sort of glorified indistinctness. This was indeed to find a prize as a prize ought to be found! That it was decrepit was its chief value, because had it not been so we could never have secured it; and the dilapidation could be repaired.

Then, out of another of the little Gothic doors came a man. He wore a sort of cloak and his head was topped with a mortar-board. He looked in surprise at the custodian and the trailing chest.

"What is this?" he demanded.

"An old chest thrown away," was the reply.

The proctor or don or whatever he was; he at least had authority; looked at the chest with an appraising eye and with distinct admiration. "There is some mistake," he said; "put it in my rooms."

There was really nothing in particular to say in protest; the chest belonged in Oxford if Oxford wanted it. But we really deserved it, for had we not come upon it it would have been taken out and destroyed, for it attracted the don's attention merely through being dragged along at the moment he happened to appear.

We were disappointed; but we were glad of the experience, for it showed us, more strikingly than ever before or since, how close the collector may be to securing a treasure, even in supposedly impossible places. We have so often seen the unexpected that we have come to expect it; but nothing could be so encouraging as to realise how close a collector may come to a fine and ancient chest from Oxford.

There are times when you see an article, and admire its charm, but do not acquire it because you really have enough of that particular kind of thing. Of what use is another tall clock or another sideboard if you really have no need for it! There are, indeed, some enthusiasts who cannot resist the appeal of another and another so long as they have space into which to crowd them. But that is accumulating rather than collecting; and between accumulating and collecting there is a difference. The lure of mere accumulation is strong, because of its being based upon a very strong love for the old, but the collector should realise that not only does he keep treasure from other collectors without any real advantage to himself, but that by crowding and cluttering his house he defeats the main purpose of collecting and home-making, which is, having the house look its very best—which it cannot do if antiques are jammed into every corner—or even stored like cordwood, as we know of forty four-post beds being kept! One's house ought not to look like a crowded antique shop, where it is the legitimate object to put as much as possible on view, for your house is not a shop. And so, when you see a thing you admire but for which you really have no place, you should fully feel its charm without trying to get it into your own possession.

Yet there comes the pleasant thought of three collecting households, all friends of ours, and of how they meet this difficulty without stinting themselves of the delight of buying, although each of the three houses is filled to repletion with antiques.

One, having packed into his house as much as it will hold, is continually sending things to friend after friend to keep for him till he has a bigger house, and the recipients are delighted because it gives them fine things for their own homes at the same time that they are accommodating him.

Another family, having all their house can hold and properly give place to, are putting away many precious pieces for their children; for their children will be marrying, and getting homes of their own, and by that time it will be more difficult to find choice old things than it is to-day. So a sideboard is hoarded for the son, fluted beds for daughters, little tables for the one who marries first, china for all.

The third collector, after filling his city home from the first floor to the garret with antiques, and not being at all ready to forego the pleasure of getting more, has solved the problem by building a home in the country and is rapidly filling that too!

The true collector never fails to see the charm in the possessions of fellow collectors or of any possessors who really appreciate them. It is exasperating to find people clinging to antiques with no appreciation of what they really are but with stubborn determination to hold them because other people would like to have them; but even in such cases the charm of the things themselves is felt by the collector who doesn't get them from the dog in the manger.

But there are times when you do not see the charm in things possessed by others, because those others have taken the charm out of them. We know of a house containing a number of antiques, with the rest of the furniture modern; but by an amazing ingenuity every antique has been spoiled. There is something positively uncanny about it. An exquisite old mirror had had a little of its veneer loosened; something easy to mend; but these pseudo-collectors, finding the loosening veneer, picked the mirror frame clean of all its veneer, and then painted the plain wood white! They had obtained a rare and beautiful claw-and-ball table; but its top was somewhat broken, as the tops of old tables are liable to be. It could easily have been mended; but instead, the top was taken off and thrown away and a new top was put on over those bandy-legs and claw-and-ball feet; a new top, of shiny mahogany, with a thick band of carved rope around its edge, in the style of particularly ugly Empire imitations! They had obtained something really fine in Empire; a delightful sofa, of the excellent early period of Empire; but they had taken off the back and burned it, so as to have a long seat that could be sat down upon from either side, and they courted admiration for their ingenuity! They had had a four-poster, no ordinary affair, with two of its posts plain and two carved, as was not infrequently the case in making old four-poster beds, and the two carved posts were of carved garlands and little lutes and musical instruments, graceful and of good design. Well, the side-pieces of the bed, and the headboard, they burned up, and the two plain posts and the canopy frame; they burned everything but the two fine posts, and these they stuck full of brass hooks, round and round, and put them in the hall for hatracks. Their unprepossessing modern furniture they had strictly respected; that was all untouched; it was only the things of positive beauty that they had sacrilegiously "improved." Those were things we certainly did not get and in them we just as certainly did not see charm.

One may feel a certain sympathy, now and then, for a person who mutilates an antique from very love of it; that is, to make it fit in some wall space or in a low-ceilinged room; but it is always a sad thing to do and is rarely excusable. But we know of an adorable instance of the opposite kind, for we have been in a room where a hole was actually sawed in the ceiling to make it possible for a tall old clock to stand there!—and the little brass eagle, up on the very top, spreads its wings in triumph.

Often antiques of the larger kinds are hacked and chopped, with maiming, decapitation, amputation, to get them through a doorway or up a stair. There really ought to be punishment for mayhem when it's tuum.

Ill-timed enthusiasm sometimes makes an antique become a thing you cannot get;—as, when one day an acquaintance was showing us her antiques, which were lost amid a medley of ordinary furniture. We frankly admired a particularly fine Heppelwhite chest of drawers, but without the slightest thought of its changing hands and were surprised when the owner said:

"Do you really care for things like that? I have some, as you see, but I don't think they are as nice as new things. The bureau cost me only a dollar, and if you care to send me any kind of a new bureau I'll be glad to give you this in exchange."

A new bureau was promptly promised for next day, with the remark that the exchange would be delightfully appreciated as the old Heppelwhite was so positively charming; a most impolitic enthusiasm, as we instantly recognised. And next morning, early, came a note, saying naïvely that the owner had changed her mind because "as it seems to be so desirable I think it would be wrong not to keep it myself." Never count your antiques before they are catched!

We know of a blacksmith, in the hall of whose house is a splendidly dignified chair which was used by one of the very earliest chief justices of the Province of Pennsylvania; it is not for sale, but none the less we

THE DINING ROOM: CORNICED AND PANELED TO MAKE AN APPROPRIATE SETTING, AND WITH WHITE WALLS TO GO WITH HEPPELWHITE AND SHERATON MAHOGANY.

INLAID HEPPELWHITE SECRETARY, WITH FINE OLD BRASSES
OF A LITTLE LATER PERIOD, AND ORIGINAL GLASS PANES.
THE ONE WE DIDN'T GET.

appreciate the interest of its age and dignity and history. We know of a splendid armoire of oak, inset with ebony: a "collector's specimen," in an old, old Holland inn; it was offered us for $300; a veritable seventeenth-century piece; and the fact that we could not conveniently buy it and assume the attendant packing and shipping made us none the less appreciate its charm. We know of many and many, a fine thing which we did not get but might have got; some of them are things we did not even see, as the ancient furniture of an ancient castle on the Scottish border, a fascinating old building out of a fascinating past, and with one room with the veritable memory that there King James of Scotland slept on the night before he was slain at the battle of Flodden, four hundred years ago. And we were told that the castle had within two years or so changed hands and gone into the possession of a man of coal mines, who had ordered his steward to clear out all the old things and furnish throughout with new, and that a local auction had been held—a slimly advertised and slimly attended auction—at which priceless things of olden time went for the proverbial song; and our informant spoke in particular of the very bed in which King James had slept. It looked so old and its hangings were so musty and ragged that it sold for only three shillings! And this from a room that had been shown with pride for many generations as King James's room! But we appreciated the charm of the old things described, and realised that, like missing the chest at Oxford, we were near enough to wonderful prizes to justify constant hope. For suppose—and it might just as likely have been so—suppose that we had been there two years earlier!

A certain possessor of fine things, last of her race, a possessor rather than a collector for she had never acquired anything except by inheritance, feared her friends. For her friends admired her old possessions, and therefore, as age crept on apace, she set about circumventing any possible thought that they might have of getting her things when she could no longer keep them. On the whole a kindly soul, too, always ready with sympathy and active help in case of trouble, but for some reason determined that no friend or acquaintance should ever succeed to possession of her prizes. She would not sell anything; her pride made her determined to hold her belongings to the last, and then:—

"I will make a will," she declared, to one of us, one day, and her voice was full of exaltation and exultation both; "I will make a will directing that all my household possessions shall be piled in my flower garden; my tables and chairs and bureaus and clocks and china"; her voice rang with pride at her own enumeration, "and in the presence of my executors everything shall be burned to ashes! What do you think of that!"

"Should you like to know? Well, you see, that kind

of burning will be sure to attract a crowd, and it will be so unusual that even the newspapers would devote some space to it, with pictures of you and your house and the fire—"

She flushed and gasped, "Oh, oh!—And I've been planning it for years! And I'm afraid I'll have to leave everything behind me after all!"

Every possessor of old things wonders what is best to do for the future, and many think of museums; a most excellent destination when the museum does not already have quite enough things of the kind and when the bequest will be appreciatively handled. Some museums in the Eastern cities, however, have already been given very much more than they can properly care for and are compelled to pack most of it out of sight where it is of no possible use or inspiration to any one. And although some museums are most admirably managed others are not. Merely to throw one's things at the nearest museum may be just as foolish as to make a bonfire of them; but, on the other hand, there is no finer destination than an excellent museum that needs them.

The house in which we lived before the one we now live in was a house of things we didn't get; it was on an old city street and was itself fairly old, with good staircase and the ghost of a banjo clock on one of the walls—the markings that showed that such an old clock had been there for many years—and there was a general atmosphere of the old, and we were told that two sisters had lived there for over sixty years.

We often wondered what kind of old furniture they had had; we were sure it must have been ancient; but after a year or two we moved away and forgot them.

But one day, recently, a friend was showing us her treasures, and among the chiefest was a delicate but strong and capacious secretary, a Heppelwhite, with drawers below, with fine original brasses, and doors with beautifully quarrelled glass: little panes, each one set in separately, instead of there being, as with modern imitations, one large piece with crosspieces of wood applied to the glass surface.

"I got that," said our friend, "at the breaking up of an old household. Two sisters, who had inherited many antiques, had lived together for sixty years—"

"Where was the house?"—But we were sure we knew and we did. For our friend had secured this particular treasure from the dining room—our dining room— where we had lived!

Over and over, in one form and another, there is the thing you did not get and the charm that can never be yours. Every collector feels as if there is a flat spot at the end of his nose from the times he has peered vainly against the glass of the little shop up-country whose proprietor has gone somewhere else up-country or has gone to a funeral or to a sale—gone, anyway— and the collector can only peer and peek and flatten, seeing treasures tantalisingly before him but out of reach. And it is always in some distant, difficult-to-reach place, where trains are few or motor friends hurrying you on. You peer and sigh and leave, never to return.

Then there is another sad kind of experience. You are longing for a pair of knife-boxes, or a sarcophagus wine-cooler: some rare, unusual thing: and you see it in a second-hand shop as you hurry to a steamer, and the man is away, and the boy in charge doesn't know what the owner asks; never heard him say; but has a list with every really useless thing in the place carefully priced. And you hurry on in despair to join your boat. It sometimes seems as if collecting is a series of missing things—if it were not that you so often get them!

We were driving one day along the most beautiful road in the world, from Salerno to Amalfi, through the Fra Diavolo region, where people still dress just as the stage folk used to in that attractive old opera; and now and then we were high, high above a fishing village that was tucked in between cliff and sea, and always the sheer cliff rose high, high above us, and always there was sapphire ocean merging into sapphire sky, and from time to time we passed the ancient isolated little Saracen towers clinging to the rocks, like birds on their perch—and on the little parapet of one such tower there stood a huge earthenware water jar that instantly we knew we must have.

It was some four feet high, an Ali Baba sort of jar. It was wonderful in shape, high-shouldered, smooth-curved, graceful, fascinating, strong.

Yes; it was a jar to acquire! And the woman who lived in this isolated stone nest was glad to sell and named a reasonable sum, volubly explaining that the jar represented the water system of the tiny castello, it holding all the water of the establishment, which was carried there on her head from a distant spring which she pointed out, a tiny green spot far up on the rose-mary-bearded mountain wall.

The money was paid—and then it was found that the jar, even empty of water, was of such a weight that it would be quite impossible to get it into the carriage; almost impossible to lift it at all. We were aghast. Should we have to leave it after all! And it was so altogether desirable. That the money had been paid was a mere detail; that meant that a certain sum had gone for experience, for a bargain was a bargain and the peasant woman was not to blame if we could not take away what we had bought.

Then there suddenly appeared on the scene, coming up from some mysterious staircase out of the depth of rock, an ancient woman with million-wrinkled face, wizened, excited, heated with avarice and rage. For her foolish daughter-in-law was selling the jar too cheap and to one of a race who, as they all knew, were ready to pay anything!

Our loyal driver put his arms about the jar; the old woman clutched the rim; there was antiphony of abuse and the jar rocked between them, the daughter-in-law and ourselves for a time becoming mere spectators and listeners; and it seemed as if we should never have a better opportunity to acquire a knowledge of colloquial personalities.

Pantingly, at length, the woman turned to us. The wife of her son was a foolish woman! The jar had been sold too cheap but for four times the sum we might have it!

"No; a bargain is a bargain." And at this our driver, who had not realised the impossibility of moving the jar, took a stronger grasp of it. He must have been a man born to achieve the impossible.

The old woman seized the money that had already been paid and held it toward us: "You will have to pay four times this!"

Well, there was just one thing to do, and considering that we had given up any thought of getting the jar it was really rather funny. The old woman was again told that the full sum had been paid and that a bargain was a bargain, but as she the more vehemently insisted to the contrary we took the money and left her holding the jar we couldn't get. But the memory of that felicitous jar will forever remain with us.

CHAPTER XII

THE CHARM OF KNOWING REAL FROM IMITATION

THERE are imitation antiques; of course there are imitations; but that does not make the genuine any the less desirable. That there are imitation diamonds has not destroyed the passion for real ones, and that there is counterfeit money has never affected the general desire of the world to get hold of as much good money as possible; and so it has always seemed particularly puerile to speak, as many do, of the existence of spurious antiques as a reason for not caring for the real. Nothing could in fact be more really reasonless than such a reason. The only sensible thing to do, after one realises that there are imitations in existence, is to try to recognise and avoid them.

And for those who collect at original sources and in out-of-the-way places there is not very much of the spurious met with. It may, of course, be met with anywhere, even among apparently honest surroundings, but there is no really great amount of it except among men who make an important business of the supplying of antiques, and there is much more of it in the big cities than in the little shops in the country, because there are more customers in the city shops and there is

180

constant temptation to keep up a greater supply than can be legitimately, gathered. In most of the large antique shops the majority of the articles shown are spurious, and most of them so plainly so as ought not to deceive a blind man.

The greatest of American collectors; or, rather, the American who spent more money than any other on collecting; missed one of its chiefest joys—the exquisite delight that comes from obtaining some old piece in the very surroundings where it has long been held. His was never the joy of personal discovery, the face to face talk at the place where the antique was found or owned. His way was, to learn through some agent, or perhaps through letters addressed to him and preliminarily passed upon by some secretary, of some supposedly marvellous cabinet, or unequalled chair, or splendid silver or porcelain, or almost priceless tapestry. Then, if he cared to consider the purchase of the article, he either relegated the matter to one of his agents, or, in rare cases, had the owner and its treasure come before him. That was his method, whether here in America, or during his frequent visits to foreign lands.

We do not say that he missed joy; joy he undoubtedly had, in thus showing his power and acting as the kingly man of wealth. But he altogether missed being a collector in the highest sense, although he gathered rare and costly things. There is doubtless pleasure in acting the lord and displaying wealth; pleasure in the holding of court, and making people come to the throne; but it is not a collector's joy nor the joy of collecting. And, too, the person who buys in that way misses all chance of applying some important tests as to authenticity.

For there are often cases in which the definite evidence is slight or imperfect; there are often cases in which the buyer, unless extremely expert in the differences between real and false, and, perhaps even though expert, can not be quite sure—cases in which the deciding factor is something in the immediate surroundings of the article. The assurance of authenticity of many a piece depends, finally, upon its environment and also on the opportunity to ask questions from the original owner.

To hear of a possible find, or to come upon it by accident; to examine it in place; to talk with the owner and those about him; to weigh and balance from evidence of the article itself and also of everything in connection with it—it is that which in many a case gives the practical and final knowledge as to genuineness.

To cater to this feeling for finding articles in their natural environment, false antiques are sometimes placed in out-of-the-way places, to impress by being come upon unexpectedly, and to lead the purchasers not to examine with the shrewdness and caution that they should ordinarily exhibit; but really, we have known of only a few such schemes, and we have looked widely.

Twice, we have known local small shopkeepers to exchange with city shops certain consignments of the genuine for highly polished impositions which these country men thought would vastly please their old and valued customers; and when these customers, one after another, as they entered the place, regretted that the dealer was mixing his stock of local, unrestored antiques with those interlopers, their town stock was not again replenished, for the collector who drops in upon these little places once or twice a year is a better customer in the end than the uninformed buyer who would never come again because his kind of purchase can be had in abundance in the city shop of false antiques.

A great encouragement for the spurious is that many people, pseudo-collectors, really love to be deceived or at least would just as soon be deceived as not. If they can without trouble get a "veritable" Sheraton at a shop they do not wish to be critical about it.

A very common source of mistake as to antiques comes from perfectly sincere misapprehension of another sort. A friend was pointing out, with pride, an old chest of drawers, and said: "This dates back into the seventeen hundreds. It came to my mother from my grandmother and traces back to my great-grandmother." But the chest of drawers was certainly not older than 1825, and so it was natural to inquire further, whereupon it appeared that the grandmother was born in 1803 and the great-grandmother about 1780, but that the great-grandmother died about 1840, which gave plenty of time and opportunity for her to own a chest of drawers of 1825.

Misapprehension of that character is very often met with, and another very frequent kind comes from the attaching of unquestioned history to the wrong piece; that is to say, the honest but mistaken transference of a description in an old inventory or in a will or receipt or other record, from the article to which it really applied, to another article altogether.

This kind of mistake is surprisingly common, for it can come about with such honest ease. It seems to us quite likely that the most famous chairs in America are mistakenly honoured through a mistake of this character; and by this we mean the honoured "Signers'" chairs in Independence Hall. For at once the collector notices that they are apparently of the period of 1780 to 1790 with backs and legs of a structure used by Sheraton and men of his time, and that they are very different from the Chippendale of the presiding officer, which would seem to be undoubtedly of correct pedigree. But they date back to 1735, you will be told, and there is a bill in existence, in the old provincial records, that shows they are part of the furnishings of that date. That there is a bill in evidence is true, referring to chairs for the members of the Colonial legislature; chairs with horse-hide seats, too; but that does not prove that these are the same chairs.

TWO OF THE SO-CALLED "SIGNERS' CHAIRS," IN INDEPEND-
ENCE HALL.

THE CHAIR OF THE PRESIDENT OF THE CONTINENTAL CON-
GRESS THAT VOTED THE DECLARATION OF INDEPENDENCE;
THE MOST NOTABLE CHAIR IN THE COUNTRY; IT IS A
REMARKABLE, HIGH-BACKED CHIPPENDALE.

A SIMPLE TYPE OF FOUR-POSTER; MADE AS LATE AS 1825. THIS IS A
KIND NOT INFREQUENTLY CARVED ON ITS SHAFT, BY DEALERS,
INTO EMPIRE FORM.

The period of British occupancy of Philadelphia and of Independence Hall doubtless played havoc with many things; the British could not be expected to love and honour the place where the Continental Congress had met and from which the Liberty Bell had been carried away, so as not to fall into their hands, and carried up into the interior over a route still remembered, through Quakertown. Time and foreign occupation would likely do away with the original chairs, and after the Revolution it would be natural to order a new outfit. The chairs that were in Independence Hall when Harrisburg was made the state capital were taken to that city early in the 1800's, and when new chairs were bought for the Harrisburg capitol those from Philadelphia were allowed to go out into private ownership, and at the time of the Centennial Exposition it occurred to some one, as a happy thought, that it would be a fine thing to find the Signers' chairs and put them back into Independence Hall; and a search was begun, through the law libraries, where the desks were found, and about the country in general, for this particular set of which so many have been recovered, the set that went to Harrisburg a hundred years ago. They are implicitly believed in; and if really the Signers' chairs would be precious beyond all price; and there is no doubt that there is a bill in existence for chairs—but to us it seems probable that the real chairs of the furnishing before the Revolution and at the most important day of the history of Independence Hall, were of an earlier date than these chairs; more likely a smaller form of the great high-backed Chippendale of the presiding officer, and without its double-height back; and that they were lost or destroyed—their original number was thirty-six —or so damaged during the Revolutionary years that they were replaced by chairs of the period immediately following.

Over and over again, old-time records and traditions and history are honestly misapplied; over and over again it is taken for granted that proving the truth of the record or tradition or history is the same as proving that it is actually connected with some particular article, whereas in reality it may or may not be. And it is easy for misapprehension to come to things of ordinary ownership when it may so easily come to the extraordinary.

An ardent American collector, recently meeting in England an English collector, the talk naturally fell upon collecting.

"Long ago," said the Englishman, "my father was in America and went to a place called Bordentown, where Joseph Bonaparte, the former King of Naples and of Spain, Napoleon's brother, had lived for years, and he told me of a marvellous pair of Italian marble mantels that he saw in what was the King's drawing room. They were exquisitely carved and he remembered them as in yellow-and-white marble. They would be worth a great deal of money in London, today. Do you know what ever became of them?"

Our collecting friend did not know; but being himself in Bordentown not many months afterwards—one of the extremely interesting among American towns, associated as it is with such a number of distinguished and titled French—he made inquiries. But no one could tell of the mantels. Perhaps they had stood in the first house of the King, which had been burned with practically all of its contents; but at any rate they were no longer there in Bordentown.

But just a few weeks ago—a year after our friend told of his search—a lady from North Carolina was sitting with us at our home, and said, "Were you ever in Bordentown?" adding that her grandfather had been a friend of Joseph Bonaparte, and that when the former King was about to return to France her grandfather was building a house, on Locust Street, at the corner of Twelfth, and that he had bought from Bonaparte a dinner service of Sèvres, which had been given him on becoming King of Spain, as a coronation gift, and was decorated with Spanish scenes, and two magnificent marble mantelpieces. "Much of the Sèvres is still preserved in the family, but trace of the mantels has been lost," for although they had been built into her grandfather's house, the building had long ago been acquired by the Historical Society of Pennsylvania, and had been torn down and replaced by a new and fire-proof structure.

We were much interested, after thus hearing of these splendid mantels in two different but cumulative ways, and when next in the Historical Society building made inquiry as to these Bonaparte mementoes. But no one seemed ever to have heard of them; until at length an official was found who felt pretty sure that he knew which were the precious ones, or at least he knew which came from the house torn down on that corner. One was dark and plain and packed away in the cellar, out of sight, and the other, a rather fine one, was built into one of the rooms of the new building. But even this official spoke cautiously, almost half-heartedly. And it seems probable that, even though these are from the Bordentown Bonaparte, they are not the very precious mantels; somehow, neither one nor the other impresses as so very superfine. And on the whole the episode served, at least, to illustrate how near even a great mu-seum may come to losing the connection between an important thing of the past and its precise history.

Mantelpieces happen to be one of the few things to which a collector cannot attach a label telling the par-ticulars of its acquisition and history. A museum can always set on a plate with an inscription but the private collector's markings must be out of sight, for his an-tiques are the furnishings of his house. But it is an excellent idea to glue a record on the bottom of a chair or a table or inside a drawer, giving the history of a piece so far as is known, and to varnish the labels to preserve them, or, to quote one of our own:

"This table belonged to a Revolutionary soldier, named Hart, who lived on Christian Street, near the wharf, in Philadelphia; it was given by his daughter, Mary Hart (who lived to the age of about ninety years) to my mother, who gave it to me. It has been in my possession about forty years."

This is dated May 21, 1913, and signed by the mistress of an old mansion from whom we got it. It is an excellent bandy-legged table, thirty years older than the beginning of the Revolution. The fact that it was owned by a Revolutionary soldier would not alone, however, establish its age as being as old as the Revolution.

A natural error for a beginner to make is to think that a piece is spurious because it is not precisely like his own. In collecting, a little knowledge is likely to be a dangerous thing, for it leads to hasty generalisation and to judgments with insufficient basis. With a beginning collector, recently, we came upon a big dining-table, which the beginner at once turned over to examine it on the under side. Seeing two large screw holes aiming in through the frame or bench, on a diagonal toward the top, he said, looking very severe: "You have taken something off."

"Not a thing," said the owner.

"Ah, but you must have done!" was the insistent reply.

The holes he was looking at were the holes of the countersunk screws that held the lid-boards, but he thought they were like two holes through which a rope pulled a cantilever on his own very genuine table and he thought all old tables of that period must have the cantilever ropes or else be altered ones or wholly false.

We know another beginner who owns a highboy of whose genuineness he is positive, down to every pin, every splinter, every keyhole. One day he looked inside the drawers of a specimen belonging to a famous friend. He smelt the sides of the drawers, he smelt the runners of the drawers, after pulling them out and in a few times to heat the wood—it looked so very professional!—he pulled them again, then smelt. "Not genuine!" he pronounced. "The structure of the drawers is not cedar!" Yet all that he could really deduce from this fact was that this highboy was not made exactly like his own. Had he found oak structure of the drawers (as distinguished from the face) he might have known it was probably made in England, or if of pine, probably in America, or if of fir, also probably made in England. But it was enough for him that it was not cedar, because his own was cedar.

England, it may be mentioned, cuts little or no timber, nowadays, but she used to use native oak, and some fir for inside parts, and yew and walnut. The walnut

of Europe is from the trees that yield what we call
English walnuts. The American black walnut can
be readily distinguished from it, both in wood and nuts.

It is impossible to set down definite rules for recog-
nising the spurious, but there are many points that are
gradually learned; as, that hand-made nails and tacks
should be looked for, they being recognisable by the
hammer marks that forged their heads; that old-time
brass tacks had brass shanks, instead of steel like modern ones, and that old screws had no points; that old-
time drawer-handles were tightened into place by nuts
instead of by screws and screwdriver; that mahogany
began to be used in furniture-making early in the
1700's but not freely until about 1725; that old-time
mirrors were silvered but that the silver was not covered
with dark red paint as nowadays, the silver often hanging in actual beads on the backs of old specimens; and
that wormholes are never found in mahogany—the taste
of worms, in furniture, apparently being not sufficiently
cultivated.

As to manufactured wormholes:—well, they really do
exist; some dealers have sometimes put them in to give
a deceptive appearance of age. Yet there is not much
of this particular kind of imposture. American collectors gather articles that have wormholes, if they care
enough for the articles, but they certainly do not deem
them an advantage. And for one piece with fraudu-
lently-made holes there are fifty in which the holes are

genuine. Yet some people are still telling in earnest the very, very ancient English joke of the man who described his trade as that of a "worm-eater"; meaning that he made artificial wormholes.

Drawers should always be carefully looked at to see if they are in "period" with the piece of old furniture in which they are found. The metamorphosed or assembled antique is the hardest to guard against in purchase. The earliest type of drawer had the face of the drawers a little wider on the sides, and a little deeper in height, than the holes holding the drawers, these faces therefore acting as the stops. But when veneering came in—and this, with English and American furniture, may be put down as about 1780—the veneered fronts of drawers were not strong enough to act as stops, and also it was desirable to have the immediate edge of the drawer disappear in the shelter of the drawer hole, so blocks of wood were put in at the backs of the drawers, to serve the purpose of stops, and the drawer fronts were made of exactly the size of the drawer space, without projection, the drawer edges being made of lines of protective wood with a rounded bead which sheltered the veneer thus enclosed from the scuffing of drawer action, or the edges were of inset square strips of wood showing like an inlaid line. Following these came, by the time of the late Empire, drawer fronts similar in structure but without any protection at the edges of the drawers, and these have usually been chipped at the corners and edges by the wear and tear of years of pulling open and pushing shut.

A very common kind of imposture is that which makes a plain old piece into one that is elaborate in shape and ornament; the tests of age are there, for the article is really old, and the imposture is often peculiarly hard to recognise. Many a plain four-poster has been reeded into Sheraton value, many a chest of drawers has had fluted corners inserted (put in sometimes with betraying wire brads), many a plain tiptable has been gouged into an apparently precious piecrust (a still cruder and cheaper way being to glue on the imitation pie-crust, as is the way with reproduction processes), many a smooth bandy-leg has had a shell-carving cut into it, thus enhancing its market price though not its distinction, many a slat-back chair without an "egg"—an egg being a charming bulbousness in the centre of the rung—has very easily had a rung with an egg put in. Every genuine egg chair, a century and a half old, shows some degree of flattening of the rounding surface of this egg, from use, and this can of course be imitated by a vigorous sandpapering on the upper side to represent the wear of heels and toes, but as a matter of fact the deceiver does not usually go to that trouble and so, in this class of case, his work is readily recognisable; this being an instance where a few minutes' work on a lathe falsely raises the value of a chair to about double.

Putting claw-and-ball feet on articles not as old as claw-and-ball period is a common form of imposition, especially in desks; and, by an odd freakishness, ogee feet, just as old as claw-and-ball, and often finer and of more graceful, more restful aspect, are taken off for claw-and-ball substitution.

A time-honoured type of imposition is that of the landlady in "Trilby," who sold to the Laird a clock given to Madame de Pompadour by Louis the Eleventh (not even the trouble to name the right Louis!). But there are always buyers ready to be sold.

A common thing, in selling grandfather's clocks, is not to call attention to the drawback if they are not eight-day clocks but one-day clocks, and the buyer never doubts their being the more costly and convenient eight-day. Once in a while, though, the buyer discovers that he has got more than he bargained for instead of less; as, one who bought a grandfather's clock, just because it was particularly good-looking, and then found that it was an eight-day clock, that it had brass works and kept good time (instead of wooden works that cheapen a clock in value and seldom run well after their years of wear), that the phases of the moon were in reasonable order, and that the hours were beautifully struck on a resonant bell. He congratulated himself on having a remarkable clock with every possible good point—and then, one day, discovered something that even the dealer had not known of; for, investigating a little hole in the side of the hood, he found traces of a string, and putting a little more length on it and drawing it through to the outside, found that the clock was a repeater and when the string was pulled would strike over again the hour last struck. This unusual clock, bought within the past year for twenty dollars, is the only one we have seen that has this repeating feature.

The single chair that goes into a cabinet-maker's shop and comes out as six chairs is illustrative of another phase of imposture, for it gives some portion of veritable old wood to every chair and also makes a prized set:—six matched chairs selling for much more than six times the price of one chair, just as six chairs and two armchairs would mount to still higher proportions; the assurance probably going with them that they are veritable and have only been restored.

Some impostures are positively amusing, and even extraordinary, as, that of the decorator who will gladly furnish you with artificial ancestors. What a first aid to the ambitious! Should you wish a line of old family portraits for your Georgian dining-room, how bootless would the wish at first thought seem! Should you wish some grim Puritans for your old-English hall, what artist could you secure! Yet the decorator steps bravely in and furnishes them. He will give you old-looking pictures in frames of ancient black or of faded gilt—cold and formal Puritans if you have outfitted in lines of austerity, or artificial ancestors bewigged and beruffled if your house is more luxuriant. He will tell you, indeed, that the English eighteenth-century figures are far more decorative than the American, on account of the richer dress, and that really, therefore, it is better to have English ancestry of that period than of those that came over in the *Mayflower*.

"I have an artist," we remember a decorator saying, "who can reproduce an antique family portrait in a way that will bring tears to your eyes."

We have an old friend, the owner of a three hundred year old house in Scotland, who possesses a beautifully mounted and engraved powder horn to which he attaches great value, because he believes it to have been carried by Charles Edward, romantically known as the "Young Pretender," in the campaign of 1745. He points out, in proof, what in reality condemns it, the letters C. E. R.—"Charles Edward, Rex," he says, proudly. But even had English royal custom permitted a king or a claimant king to cognomen himself with two names before the Rex, this inscription would still be fatal, for in 1745 Charles Edward made no claim whatever to the kingship but was heading a rebellion for his father, who was still alive.

But somehow, an obvious imposture seems to be quite as successful as a cleverly concealed one; people are so ready to be deceived.

The old-furniture lover who would not be deceived

must in the end come to rely upon something more than tests and knowledge, for there comes into play, in the course of years, a trained skill that is really a sort of instinct; but he must needs be careful, in trusting to this instinct, which comes as the result of long study, observation and experience and a real love for the genuine old, that he should never let himself become, in the delightfully forceful ancient words, "wiser in his own conceit than seven men that can render a reason."

And surely that irreverent versifier was a lover of old furniture, who wrote: "The murmuring pines and the hemlocks, planed and veneered, in coats of shellac and new varnish, stand like Chippendale highboys, with drawers brass-handled and polished."

CHAPTER XIII

THE CHARM OF COLLECTING ONLY THE WORTH WHILE

WE knew a dear old clergyman, long since dead, who, returning from the one journey of his life to Palestine, somehow managed to bring back with him a grievous burden of stones; just ordinary stones from the fields or highways, but one from every place of note that he had visited in the Holy Land; and the places and the stones were many, for he had gone with a devout heart and a memory into which was packed familiar and unfamiliar names.

He got the stones home, and managed to label most of them, though from the first they were recalcitrant as to glue or paint or gum. He used to describe the stones to callers, naming one by one the places from which so burdensomely they had been carried, but he could not fail to note a certain lack of attention on the part of his people, although he had been accustomed to find them interested in whatever he did or said. So after a while he ceased to show the stones. For a while longer he tried to go over them by himself, but was surprised and grieved to find that they were no longer arousing either the traveller's or the religionist's glow. "This stone is from the roadside in Bethlehem," "This was picked up in a field near the home of Joseph"—such words, which had early begun to pall upon his flock, began to lose their zest for even himself. Being a sensible man, he thereupon set himself to find the explanation, and being also a wise man, he found it; and it was, that the stones had no essential interest or value. They were old, and therefore might have been expected to have the charm of age; and they were from famous places, thus adding the possible charm of association; but that they possessed neither good looks nor use was their fatal lack. They were neither beautiful nor utilitarian. They were merely uninteresting stones. And a thing of age which has neither distinction nor beauty is really not worth while.

Then he put the stones to serve at least a useful purpose, for, taking off such descriptive marks as had not hopelessly fallen off, he indiscriminately used them as the pavement of a path to his flowers.

These stones were clearly without intrinsic interest or value, but there are often articles much more difficult to judge, articles without real beauty or value yet possessing a certain amount of definite interest, as distinguished from the indefinite. The antiquary who "shows on holidays a sacred pin that touched the ruff that touched Queen Bess's chin," has a certain excuse for his collecting, although not very much unless the pin was in itself worth while—as it very likely was if that imperious dame really wore it. But this kind of collecting, in which the interest is dependent upon some personal association, can never be of the highest class and is certainly not at all of the kind that fills one's home with things intrinsically worth while.

But, as to what is worth while in collecting, there can be no hard and fast rule. There will be differences in judgment so long as there are differences in personality. To some, a Chippendale chair is worth while and to others it isn't. One may, of course, quote the opinions of many persons of accepted taste, but even with this it is impossible to make out so clear a case as can fortunately be made out for, say, such a painting as the Mona Lisa. As to that, when you find some one fleering, you can say, not only that at the time it was painted its immense value was recognised by the man of finest taste in Europe, the royal Francis, but that continuously, since then, the best taste of the world has upheld that judgment, even through that long period which so objurgatively keeps in memory the time of Victoria. But as to fine old furniture the case is different. There was a long period when there was none so poor to do it reverence; or, if reverenced, it was apologetically if not even secretly. There was Oliver Wendell Holmes, that man of fine culture and of taste and tradition; he could not help seeing the charm of the old, and he wrote feelingly of old family portraits and furniture and silver. He loved the old furniture which

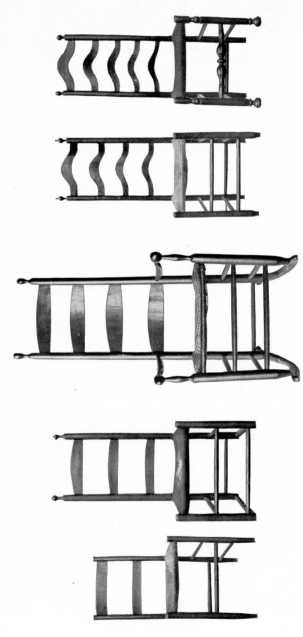

FIVE TYPES OF SLAT-BACK CHAIR, RANGING FROM 1750 TO 1825. THIS FIVE-SLAT ARE THE MOST SOUGHT FOR. THIS FIVE-SLAT HAS KNOB FEET, AND DOUBLE-EGG ON RUNG.

AN EMPIRE SOFA, OF ABOUT 1815, OF UNUSUALLY GOOD LINES AND PROPORTIONS. IT HAS THE TYPICAL ACANTHUS LEAF AND WINGED-CLAW.

the taste of his time was scorning. Yet his love was
shamefaced and humble, for, as he expressed it, he
thought it well for a man to keep his claw-footed chairs
and black mahogany tables and bevel-edged mirrors
and stately upright cabinets—if he had "some old
place" to keep them in! They were not to be kept with
pride, as things of daily use, but to be put into some
distant corner if the owner had such a corner, the implication necessarily being that if he had no such distant and forgotten spot the only thing to do was to destroy them. When a man with the training and traditions of Oliver Wendell Holmes was impressed to that
extent by the spirit of his age, small wonder that the
world in general was similarly impressed.

We know an enthusiastic collector, whose home is
filled with fine things of the past, who tells of how, in
her girlhood, the taste was so antagonistic to what is
now so honoured and loved, that there was nothing to
do with a charming claw-footed table which had come
down to her, but to throw it away; the family home had
no place for it; whereupon, not being willing utterly to
destroy it, she had it made into a mirror frame, which
she describes with mingled amusement and horror at the
memory but with somewhat of justifiable pride that even
in the Dark Ages of taste she loved the beautiful. It
is matter of amazement that so much of the old was
saved, but there were fortunately garrets, and there
were country homes to which the wave of bad taste did

not penetrate, and there were owners who fortunately could not afford to throw things away, and there were a few people who, although with shamefacedness, tucked the precious old things safely out of sight, where they have waited for national emergence from the tidal wave of bad taste.

When practically everybody, only a few years ago, united in devotion to false gods of furniture, it is not surprising that there are still quite a number who do not join in the collectors' enthusiasm for the fine things of the distant past; and to such persons no direct argument can be offered, for it is a matter of taste.   The familiar and jibingly-intended phrase, "It's all in your eye!" really fits the case; of course it is all in your eye; for you have either the right kind of eye or the wrong kind of eye.

A critical friend said to Whistler, one day, that a certain painting was not good, to which Whistler replied, blandly: "Don't say it's not good.   Say you don't like it.   Then you'll be safer."

Of course, in criticising and discarding and altering, there should be avoidance of what some one has well termed æsthetic egotism; but at the same time collectors ought to have the courage of their convictions after they have tried to make their convictions worth while.   The Florentine artist—it is old Vasari who tells of him— who refused to look at an offered crucifix, when dying, because it had been too poorly carved, stands for the over-particular; and yet one admires the spirit that demands the right thing or none.

In connection with what is worth while, the question will often be asked, why a reproduction of the old is not as excellent as the old itself? And if it were really a reproduction, it would be as good, except—but this is a great exception!—that it does not possess the powerful charm of association with the past. And this is far from a fanciful charm. It is a feeling deep-based in human nature, a feeling that has always been powerful and whose satisfaction has given keen and intelligent joy, an exquisite and very real pleasure.

But, more than this, there is seldom a perfect reproduction. The furniture that collectors love was made by hand-working artificers whose skill cannot be imitated by machinery. The old-timers "wrought with loving care," and with great skill. The hand-made furniture of to-day cannot rival that of the past in execution because there has been no training of artificers for generation after generation; they flew out of the window when machinery came in at the door, and they cannot return without generations of training and an atmosphere of appreciation. And, still worse, most of the reproductions of to-day are made by machinery and so are entirely without the merits that come only from hand work.

And the matter of copying comes in. The copy needs to be exact. But few makers or designers of to-day are either able or willing to copy exactly. They just miss a curve here, and add a line there, and alter proportion somewhere else. They "improve"!—they "adapt"!

It was a curious experience, one day, to go through the great warehouse of a concern whose specialty is the making of copies of the old: not to sell as pretended originals but frankly as reproductions. The manager showed room after room filled with things just a little wrong—but how very, very important that little was! —and, last thing of all, we came to a room in which were kept old-time originals, the charming things which they had almost copied but had spoiled in the copying; and he threw open the door with a flourish which plainly showed how insignificant, to him, were these originals when compared with the ones that had just been shown; how superior and patronising was his state of mind toward those originals.

Proportion is one of the most subtle of qualities, and line and colour are subtle; and almost always, with a reproduction, line is a mocker, wrong shape is raging, and, to quote the rest of the sentence literally, whosoever is deceived thereby is not wise.

In the general matter of collecting old furniture it is quite impossible to say precisely what is or is not worth while. Standards from collectors, to collectors, and for collectors must necessarily vary according to particular needs. Always, one should keep up his gauge of distinction, get as excellent examples as he can, and collect only what can be used or shown to advantage in his home.

It may often be that what is worth while for one person is not worth while for another. An outfit of old kitchen utensils, wrought by blacksmiths of long ago, is fascinating in some old kitchen of a house that stood before the Revolution but would be out of taste and place in a city apartment. An acquaintance recently relinquished the opportunity to acquire a great Dutch Kaas because it would not go well with his house, whose rooms were small, nor with his furniture, which in general type was fragile and slender. The Dutch Kaas simply would not have harmonised and he had the strength of mind to let it go.

Ordinarily, however, that an antique is not precisely the same style as the antiques already in possession is no disadvantage, for articles of different periods, if not of too widely different character, fall into pleasant harmony and may be more effective than when in absolute similarity in period, room by room. The world finds that chairs of different periods can sit peaceably near each other and not offend.

Freaks are among the things distinctly not worth while, and of freaks there are many kinds. A collector went to visit an old lady who had sent word that she would like him to see some valuable old pieces, "absolutely original relics," and he found her treasures to be only a gilded chair made of three spinning wheels and a settee made of a bedstead! There is nothing to say in the presence of such things except the words that Lincoln loved to use: "It seems to me that for people who like that sort of thing, it is just about the kind of thing they would like." This old lady, by the way, really did possess something worth while—an excellent chair, unaltered, but utterly abased and disregarded and only used to set the milk bottles on at the back door. Naturally there was a suggestion of her disposing of this chair, so evident was it that she did not value it herself, but she would not listen to the suggestion from one who had shown no wish to buy what she called her "spinning chair."

It seems strange, nowadays, to realise that it was not many years ago that the ideal of many a person who aspired to be thought a lover of the old, was a spinning wheel; not made into something else like the three wheels and the gilded chair, but kept in its original and proper shape, except that it was probably, by the truly esthetic, touched up with a little enamel paint and a pink ribbon. The wheel, with hank of flax attached, stood in many a parlour as the outward and visible sign of taste. Ten dollars apiece was thought a proper price, but now their glory has departed. Not long ago, we came upon a dealer in a country town, who, in trying to corner the spinning wheel market in his neighbourhood, just as the demand was beginning to decline, had bought a large number of them but now would be glad to sell them for twenty-five cents apiece or even to give one away as a sort of premium with the sale of other things, if the buyer should care enough for one to take it along for nothing.

And this shows how readily taste may swing from one extreme to another. As a matter of fact, although a spinning wheel was always absurd as an ornament for a modern sitting room, it does, after all, serve to preserve an interesting touch of old-time ways, and finds a felicitous place in a garret.

What joy there is in the very thought of a garret! There is the charm of accessible seclusion, of dim and dusky remoteness, of a ceiling that slopes delightfully down. An upper floor that is finished off in absolute brightness, with bedrooms and bathrooms and billiard room, is not a garret! The real garret is never bright, and it is always rather crowded; and garrets are especially endeared to lovers of the past because it was there that many, many antiques took refuge from the Goths and Vandals.

A garret appeals to the imagination both of the old and the young, and in that lies its greatest of all delight—its appeal to the imagination. The other day we saw two children, a boy and a girl, descendants of a Revolutionary worthy, enter an old garret, and it was the first garret in which they had ever been. Instantly, it became for them an enchanted land; instantly they began searching and discovering such things as dreams and stories are made of, and in this they were experiencing a joy that is similarly felt by all ages, for the appeal of the garret is broad.

Primarily and properly for storage, a garret should also be for more than that. In our garret, which is mentioned merely as an example of what any collector's may contain, there is necessary storage space but there is a spot near the window which forms a garret room. There is a table there, and there are several chairs, one of them, an Empire wooden chair, simple but of excellent shape, having been picked up in Alexandria, in the very house in which General Braddock and six Colonial governors met to talk over the coming campaign. In that house the very room is shown; a once-splendid room, with cornice, pilasters, panels and pediments. The chair being Empire, does not date back to within half a century of the time of that historical meeting.

And what a splendid old house it was! It is given over to devastation and decay, now, but its magnificent stair, and its corniced rooms, and its roof with dormers and balustrade, and its stone-arch-supported terrace looking out over the Potomac, are eloquent of the glories of the past, and one hopes that the plans, discussed by a patriotic society, for rehabilitating it, will be carried out. Washington met Braddock in this house, and in it his commission as a British officer was offered and accepted. Nathaniel Hawthorne tells somewhere of

THE SHADOWY OLD GARRET.

THE SECLUDED SUNKEN GARDEN, WITH OLD SUN-DIAL.

being in an English city, and seeing a British regiment
go marching by on its way to the Crimean war with its
torn and faded old colours proudly flying, and of being
told by a British friend that one of the proud boasts of
that regiment was that it had the name of George Washington on its rolls.   "I never heard of that before," com-
ments Hawthorne.

Throughout his life, Washington was a frequent and
welcome guest in this old Alexandria house, the Carlyle
house as it is known, and one cannot help realising that
if such a house were in England, with its remains of
grandeur and its associations with Washington and
Braddock and a host of other great folk of the early
days, it would be eagerly visited by throngs of Americans, whereas in America it has been almost completely
neglected.

The house was almost bare of everything when we
were there three years ago; the original furnishings had
disappeared decades before; but this old chair was there
and the owner wanted merely a dollar for it, which certainly shows that he was making no effort to sell at high
prices to dazzled visitors!

In our garret is a little keg, also from Alexandria;
as old as the time of Washington, this, but with no association either with him or the Carlyle house; it is only
that it was found in this town, which was the metropolis
of that part of Virginia in those early days, and that it
is well worth having in itself; it is of only three-pint

capacity and only seven and a half inches high, it is of delightful oval shape instead of round, and it is delicately made of tiny staves of oak, bound round with eight hoops of brass; a fascinating miniature keg, very old, and with a flavour not only of age but of the oldest of Bourbon.

The garret is the place for things that are not quite the best or that are too much worn-out, or things that really do not seem to belong anywhere else; it is a flotsam and jetsam sort of a place.

We have in this old garret a slat-back chair from a New England village—from a New England garret right to ours—a chair with three slats, and therefore of more interest than one of only two slats but not of so much value as one of four slats would be or the rarer five, which is uncommon indeed. We have never seen a six-slat, and do not think such a thing exists, but it may. This three-slat is not at all to be classed among the worth while for sending any distance, and it came to us through a misunderstanding, but is kept as a pleasant memento of a pleasant place.

There is a rather dilapidated rush-bottom chair acquired within less than a mile of our home; it had no rush in it when we got it, so was a rush-bottom only by courtesy. Getting it so near at hand had made it worth while to gather.

There is a spinning wheel; for this is a garret, and a spinning wheel always seems part of an old garret. It

comes from the vanishing Shakers, this, those picturesque, persevering, hardworking folk—such a quiet
folk, too, in spite of their stirring name!—who founded
communities and built great buildings and farmed great
farms but could not attract the converts necessary to
keep in existence a celibate sect.   This wheel was one
of our very earliest acquisitions, and bears an old label,
put on by us at the time, saying that it was "made and
used by the Shakers of North Union, Ohio, and obtained from them at their village"; a village that years
ago disappeared from existence.

Upon the wheel hangs the ancient gourd, in which
the Shaker women used to dampen their fingers for
handling the flax, and the hank of flax itself is on a distaff, made with remarkable skill, solid at top and bottom, with open work of six radiating lines of wood, the
whole being of one undivided piece of some extremely
tough wood.   And how curious it is that the distaff, for
ages standing as the symbol of woman and womanhood,
has almost passed not only out of use but out of knowledge!

There is a comfortable old sofa in the garret, not
quite good enough for downstairs, and there is a tall
three-legged skillet with its handle long enough to be
used, in supping, with the proverbial long-handled
spoon, and there is a skep, a bee-hive, of typical ancient
shape, a shape quite forgotten in these days of boxes
for bees.   The skep is from an old farmhouse of the

curious sect of Dunkards, and is a curiously oval sort of basket, marvellously made with twisted ropes of straw going round and round and bound together with long strings of rush. Here it stands open end up, for use as a paper-basket, but when the bees used it this open end was down, and the skep was fastened upon a bench or board by a heavy ear of leather, which permitted of turning the skep up to cut out the honeycomb. Standing on its board, the skep had the funniest kind of a little door, right at the board level, just big enough for a good fat bee to enter—in fact, the size of the door, in relation to the size of the skep, is about the same as the size of the small door that is the main entrance of the Capitol at Washington in relation to the size of the great building itself. And from the skep there still comes a delicious, wholesome odour of beeswax. Some day this will again be out in a garden and have bees in it.

There is an old bellows for the wood stove, there is a pewter inkwell, found in Dundee, and with four holes for sticking in the old quill pens, there is a three-legged fireside crane, from an old inn, for holding a kettle over an open fire, there are several chests of pine or of oak used for the practical putting away of clothing, between seasons, and there is a little low travelling chest, a rounded-top hair-trunk, studded with brass nails, a trunk which made the journey, in the long ago, in an ox cart, from Connecticut to the Western Reserve.

Really the possibilities of even a garret are endless.

There is an old-time lantern, and there are candle-sticks, and there are scissor-like snuffers, besides a couple of cone-shaped extinguishers; those little caps that just fit over the candle-top and instantly extinguish the flame without smoke—little pointed night-caps; and of these one is of copper, quite unusual, from the Western Reserve, excellently made, but with a certain prim severity, and the other is from Holland and of the customary brass; and in shape they are precisely alike and each has its little ring handle on the side.

There is a candle-mould, of tin, which was brought home from a walk on the Scotch hills from a cottage by the roadside, and it is precisely similar to candle-moulds, of tin, that may still be found in the garrets of American farmhouses.

And on the wall hangs an old-time coach horn, five feet in length, a horn that used to be blown from the top of an old-time coach. Of a sonorousness, is the sound of this horn—the kind of horn that echoes through the centuries preceding railways, and which has vanished quite away. Ah, well, how things have changed, how completely has the new order replaced the old! And how odd it would be if the ghost of some coach guard should pass over these modern roads, and how puzzled he would be and how his ghostly heart would stir, for everywhere he would read the friendly admonition: "Blow your horn!"

CHAPTER XIV

THE CHARM OF SPECIALISING

WE know of a house which is furnished so perfectly as to remain in the memory as an unusually fine example of what a collector may do. There is old-time furniture; there are Heppelwhite, Chippendale, Adam; but in addition to this, and what gives the house unique distinction, the walls of the drawing room, the library and the hall are hung closely about with old mezzotints. None are put away in portfolios and drawers; they all hang on the walls as the principal feature of the furnishing of the house; and although ordinarily so many pictures would give the effect of sadly overcrowding, here their charm and mellowness make the rooms of remarkable beauty and restraint. The walls are tinted a deep creamy white, making a fine background for the old mezzotints in their narrow black frames; the curtains are of a quiet mossy green; the furniture is highly waxed and very dark:— every detail is thought of to obtain the best accompaniment of this kind of picture.

Mezzotints such as these, made by old-time artists from the portraits painted by Gainsborough, Reynolds, Raeburn and their cotemporaries, are so altogether charming that it is a pity that the art of the mezzotinter has gone; but it was too expensive a method to withstand competition with modern photographic processes, and so a fascinating kind of picture has practically or altogether ceased to be made.

Not only is there this specialisation in mezzotints in the house of which we spoke, but there is the further detail that much more attention has been given to the gathering of mezzotints of women than of men; but this came in some degree from the fact that the eighteenth century artists more often painted the court and society beauties than they did their husbands.

This collector of old furniture with mezzotints as a specialty, found his task easier because his collection was begun by his father, who educated him in the knowledge of fine things and bequeathed him the beginning of the collection; and gaining a knowledge of fine things, and in particular of some special branches, is in itself the finest kind of specialising.

The joy of life is so greatly increased by any increase of special knowledge in regard to the fine things of life, that every collector finds it worth striving for. Possession of very much is not absolutely necessary, no matter how very satisfactory it might be; but special knowledge, and making oneself an authority as an expert, is always its own delightful reward.

Every collector is sure to specialise, in some degree; he is sure to favour Chippendale or Empire or Wedgwood or something; and if he not only favours them but gains special knowledge in regard to them and gathers excellent examples of them as near the very best as he can, he finds an added delight, an added intelligence, in collecting. And it is not, in general, the total number of specimens that counts, so much as the excellence of the specimens, their representative qualities, and a really understanding acquaintance with them and with their making.

The great danger of specialising is that it is liable to degenerate into hoarding, storing, mere accumulating; when a man like one we know of packs thirty-eight four-posters into his garret, stacking them like cord wood, he may call himself a specialist in four-posters, but he is even more a hoarder; those four-posters really do him very little good, and there is a distinct selfishness in keeping them from others. That general type are the misers of old furniture.

But it all depends. Getting a large number of one particular kind of thing may be excellent as collecting, or it may be reprehensible. It depends on the kind of article, and the spirit behind the collecting, and the way in which the collection is handled. No one could think of criticising the mezzotint collector, for every picture is used so beautifully and the owner is so well-informed an enthusiast that he and his collection become exponents of this whole form of engraving; the ideal conditions for collection and collector.

THE LURE OF LUSTRE: THE RESULT OF A YEAR'S SPECIALIZING IN COPPER LUSTRE, ROSE LUSTRE, SUNDERLAND LUSTRE, AND SILVER LUSTRE.

A HEPPELWHITE HIGH CHEST-OF-DRAWERS, INLAID WITH EBONY, AND
WITH ORIGINAL BRASSES AND EXCELLENTLY DESIGNED FEET.

The particular locality in which one lives may suggest a specialty; as in the case of that collector of the Western Reserve who makes a point of gathering things that went there in the early days from Connecticut, and this collector has knowledge of inventories, wills, family records and old letters bearing on the early household histories of his neighbourhood. We know of another collector who gathers only antiques from New England, not letting herself be tempted with even the most beautiful things from old England or from other parts of our own country.

Without aiming at one kind to the exclusion of all other kinds, one may at least gradually make his collection tend in particularly desirable directions, and by so doing begin to enjoy the *fin fleur* of collecting. Our own special taste is for Heppelwhite, and each acquisition of another piece in this style is a positive joy. The table, preciously inlaid, that we have had only since last December, gives a satisfaction far beyond that of its beauty alone; there are felicitous sidetables, almost a pair; there is the sideboard that was the first of our Heppelwhite possessions; there are tea-caddies in his beautifully inlaid designs; there is the loveliest of all, so we believe—a piece, all of satinwood, bought, "unsight, unseen," as with the treasures of childhood, away down South, on the description and pencil sketch of a friend, and it is the source of great anticipatory collecting happiness.

Our second love is for Chippendales, and of his style of chair we already have six that are undoubtedly genuine old examples, and each chair was obtained in a different way and place. Thus they all have, for us, delightful attractiveness besides that which comes from age and beauty. Yet we do not think of ever having only Heppelwhite or Chippendale alone; to us, that would seem a great mistake, an unnecessary limiting of one's pleasures without a compensating gain, for there are so many, many delightful things that can be used in a house, and even the most persevering of collectors cannot hope to get enough of them of one style exclusively. And fortunately the different styles of the latter half of the eighteenth century give a sense of harmony when they stand together in the same room.

With china it is the same as with furniture; it is excellent to tend toward specialties, without holding oneself to one variety alone. If a collector loves the Chinese Lowestoft, favoured by early American households, that is no reason why he should bar himself from the beauty of American-made Tucker! Though he is enthusiastic for Staffordshire, that is no reason why he should ignore an opportunity to get the excellent Bennington!

There is a very real charm about blue Staffordshire, with its English-made views of American scenes; and it has become a pleasure to us to get together considerable of it; enough, indeed, to serve a dinner with old blue;

but we should not think of cutting ourselves off from other attractive kinds.

We love—as who does not!—the fine old Sèvres, and we have been so fortunate as to gather a few beautiful pieces, and hope to gather more; but that has not kept us from getting other porcelain and earthenware as well; and just as the satisfying of a fancy we have yielding to the lure of lustre, and have managed to collect many pieces of that attractive old ware, including not only the familiar copper lustre, in varied shapes and sizes, but some of rose lustre and silver lustre, and even a half dozen examples of the odd, rosy, speckled lustre of Sunderland. Somebody once declared, very boastfully, that he took all learning to be his province; but the collector may say, not at all boastfully, that he takes all old furnishings and furniture to be his province.

In specialising, there is many a curious variant. A grandmother with one grandchild, having collected a town house, a country house and a place in Maine, and filled them all rather heterogeniously, found the greatest joy of her life in specialising in toy furniture. Miniature four-posters, so perfect as to make one sure they were models and not playthings, chests, desks, cradles, chairs, double-chairs, tables, high chests and low, andirons, kettles, little silver coffee pots with ebony handles—she has eagerly gathered them all, and she points with appreciation to how carefully and lastingly they are made as compared with the playthings made for children to-day.

She has gathered sufficient to show a complete history of furniture, in miniature, from the year 1600 down to 1825, and it makes a very interesting study. We ourselves can count almost forty pieces of miniature furniture that we have seen, at places widely distant, and possible of acquirement for similar specialisation.

Special collecting of costumes has an appeal to artists, who delight in the colours and the grandeur of old brocades and glorious adornments; and hundreds of them are acquiring such treasure for their studios.

Old bead bags have been one of the interesting minor things to collect, and we know an up-country dealer who always says, delightfully unconscious that his word is an odd one, an old survival, that he has "seft" (meaning "saved") all the bead bags he has for one certain "bead-bagger," a collector who comes to him often. This collector takes a keen interest in bead bags; the kind of interest that ought to be taken in any specialty; for she has studied the old-time ways of making them, and has many of the formulas by which the beads were strung, as, so many white, so many green, then a ruby and a white, then two green; all the beads, thousands of them, having been strung on the silk thread before the knitting began and then one by one slipping over the needle and falling into pattern automatically. Exquisite bead-making this, giving soft flexibility and result-

ALMOST A MATCHED PAIR OF GRACEFUL INLAID SIDE-
TABLES: TYPICAL HEPPELWHITE DESIGN.

A GOOD TYPE OF PLAIN HEPPELWHITE DESK, WITH
BRACKET FEET.

FOUR EARLY FIRE INSURANCE EMBLEMS, SUCH AS ARE STILL
TO BE FOUND ON OLD HOUSES.

ant in surfaces all of beads, not silk, the thread being completely hidden. Such intelligent and successful specialisation is far from mere accumulation—it is an effort to show the complete field of possibilities, with an old-time artistic handicraft.

There are such differences in specialising—it may be a kind that is wise or it may be really not worth while—after all, it depends upon individual circumstances quite as much as upon individual taste; and there comes, in illustration of view-points variant, the collecting of the insurance emblems that used to be put upon the fronts of insured houses; not the homely tin things into which they gradually deteriorated, but the good-looking, old-fashioned emblems of the time when pretty nearly everything was good-looking. Most of the old-time ones are castings, some of them mounted upon oak plates or shields; and there was the green tree, emblem of the insurance company brave enough to insure houses with trees about them, at a time when the other companies ordered nearby trees cut down as a condition precedent; and there was the four clasped hands making a square, a fascinating emblem; and there was the old-fashioned hand engine, with snaky hose, and there were many more, such as are still to be seen *in situ* on the fronts of many old Philadelphia and Boston houses.

Our friend has only two or three of his fire-emblem treasures at his home; more than that would not be effective in a house, even though, like his, it is filled with antique belongings.   With the others, he lined the walls of his office; and as he is an insurance man this is a peculiarly fitting thing to do with them.   It is ideal specialising.

Not long ago he was in England, and a certain lord over there, with the reputation of having the best fire-emblem collection in England, was anxious to meet him. Now, there was no reason at all why that lord should care for fire insurance emblems; but idle collecting is a very general occupation for the idler, over there, and he was merely the kind who gathers like a magpie, just for the sake of gathering.   And the insurance man himself felt this and was impatient with it; he knew that there was no collector's fellow-feeling on the part of the Englishman; and being very busy during his few days in London, he treated very cavalierly a number of pressing telephone messages from the fire-emblem lord, and it amused him hugely to notice with what awe he was treated, in that ultra-English hotel, as a man who actually dared to slight the advances of a member of the nobility!

CHAPTER XV

THE CHARM OF AUCTIONS

THE two kinds of acquisition that are furthest apart in character are acquisition by auction and acquisition by inheritance; one kind representing no judgment at all and the other representing judgment that must needs be instantaneous.

It is really delightful to acquire, by inheritance, the beginning of a collection, or thus to add to a collection already begun, for there is not only the beauty of things themselves, with the veritable touch of the past—the smack of age, the relish of the saltness of time—but there comes at the same time a feeling of proper pride that the articles are from one's ancestors.

Yet there are times when one is tempted to look upon the inheritance of antiques as a misfortune, for it is so liable to give an unenlightened self-complacency. We have all met the people who, inheriting from ancestors of taste, do not even take the trouble to find out why the treasures should be treasured, except that they hear of connoisseurs and collectors treasuring them.

The pride of some folk in antique possession which they have inherited, but which they are quite incapable of intelligently adding to—the pride of such persons in the fact that the good taste of the family ended with the lives of their ancestors—is really extraordinary; or, to quote an excellent distinction drawn by the celebrated Mr. Jingle in a certain conversation with the even more celebrated Mr. Pickwick, "not extraordinary, but singular."

There was an auction that we call the cent auction; it was at a farmhouse whose owner had died, leaving his little belongings to be inherited by distant and well-to-do relatives he had never seen, and perhaps a general knowledge of this fact kept down the bids; but however this may have been, there was little enough to tempt, in any case, and of that little only a small part was antique, and none of it had ever been highly valuable.

And the bids began with a cent! Quite a number of things were sold for that, and when the auctioneer began putting things in little "lots" it did not alter matters. Amused competition now and then raised a price to three cents or four. The sense that they would not bid had permeated the people; it was a sense of humour, following the unspoken determination not to swell a fund for the inheriting stranger—a sort of loyalty to their old neighbour! Now and then a one-cent bid secured us a blue plate, with two or three homely things that had to be left behind; the pile in front of us kept growing; there was a blue Canton vegetable dish, there were dark blue, pale blue and old pink plates, and a bid of one cent actually gave us a Lowestoft cup and saucer!

But it was another sort of experience that took one of us a railway journey of sixty miles to a country auction that promised interesting results. The house was old and the things were old, but the sale was barely more than under way when up came several motor cars, filled with dwellers at a big summer hotel a few miles away, and they were bound to buy antiques. They seemed to have little knowledge of values, and were ready to bid higher, in that distant place, where each purchase involved crating and hauling and shipping and repairing, than they would need to pay in city shops from which articles would be delivered in perfect order. It is always fair to expect lower prices when there is to be considerable expense for repairs and transportation.

The country folk stood aghast to see droopy-leaved tables with turned legs go for twenty-five dollars, and chairs of the Civil War period sell for fifteen, and the group of collectors who were present were astonished. It was evidently the method of these summer-visitors to wait until they saw some one whom they deemed a judge of antiques looking at something, whereupon they would start eagerly in and try to get the thing away from him. Ordinary painted chairs, with wooden seats, the kind with flowers on the rail and of very plain make, the kind that ordinarily sell at a sale for twenty-five cents or fifty at the most, they were quite ready to run up to five dollars; one tip-table, worth not over ten dollars, was sold to them for seventy. It was a matter for some comfort to notice that they mistakenly followed some rather misleading leads; in fact, there were chances taken for practically worthless things, by some of the collectors present, but always the summer boarder took the bait. In all it was rather an amusing afternoon, and the huge old melon basket that was bought in the sale at the dooryard to hold the old china we meant to buy but didn't, made a good garden basket afterwards.

It was a Frenchman who remarked, once upon a time, that the most fascinating thing in all the world is a key —because you never know what it is going to open! But had that Frenchman ever got into the way of attending auctions in search of antique prizes he would have put auctions ahead of keys as things of potential surprise.

One day, just a few years ago, we noticed in a New York paper an advertisement of an auction that was to take place at a house on Madison avenue, whose number showed it to be in the fine old-fashioned part below Forty-second street. The books and china and furniture were to be on view, in advance, but there was no chance to get to the house until late in the afternoon of the very day before the sale; and a dark and rainy afternoon it was, in late November.

The house was quite dark. But a caretaker, with a

candle, answered the bell, and, procuring another candle, led the way. Two men with candles peering about in that cavernous old brown stone mansion, made an odd and ghostly sight.

But the furniture was a disappointment. It towered to the lofty ceilings in grim heights of heavy ornateness. The inspection was made hastily, but it was clear that there was nothing worth while—nothing, with one exception.

That exception was upstairs, and it was something that in the dim light had seemed attractive and which, holding the candle close, proved to be that rare thing, a genuine Heppelwhite chair! But there was something odd about it, and even in the candle-light it could be seen that the oddity was that although it was an armchair it had not originally been so, but that the modern arms had been superimposed long after the chair was made.

Next day, at the auction, we were prepared to go as high as twenty-five dollars for the chair; not more than that, for it would need considerable rehabilitation, especially in connection with the taking off the arms and putting it back into its original shape. And our natural hope was that, for that one chair, disguised by false arms and red plush and dangling fringe around the seat and standing in solitary worth amid a household of costly but ordinary and ugly things, there would be little competition! But, alas! at the sale, though things of great cost of forty years ago went for almost nothing, the watchful eyes of dealers and collectors were on that particular chair and bidder after bidder appeared when it came to its turn. The altered and disguised Heppelwhite was the object of general desire, and in spite of its crippled condition it was swiftly run up, in eager competition, to sixty-nine dollars—for it was genuine, it was not beyond restoration, it would be a notably fine specimen when cleared of its arms and fringe and plush.

An auction is the very place in which to be on the lookout for some missing piece or part, to outfit some antique that is in need of it; and it is surprising how often one may find just what he desires. Lids for Lowestoft teapots, headboards for old beds, extra mahogany leaves for tables or repair work—every collector has had some wonderful experience in matching or completing some set of brass or glass or china. And an illustrative example comes to mind; an experience with a picture that we inherited, of an ancestor with frilled shirt and other picturesque points. He came without a frame and for three years we waited vainly for the proper frame, hoping for an antique, in gold, with designed corners and smooth-curved sides. Then at an auction we saw two plain frames of wood, dark with age. They were probably some eighty years old. For ten cents they became ours—and one of them was just the frame for the ancestor! To be sure, it wasn't precisely

A FOUR-POSTER THAT COST TWENTY-FIVE CENTS AT A RE-
CENT NEAR-BY AUCTION; PICTURESQUE BUT NOT VALU-
ABLE; IT ORIGINALLY HAD A CURVING CANOPY.

THE "SHERATON-FANCY" CHAIR, BOUGHT AT AN AUCTION
FOR THIRTY-FIVE CENTS; ALSO SIDE-CHAIR OF SAME
STYLE.

A RARE CLAW-AND-BALL TABLE, OF THE MIDDLE OF THE
EIGHTEENTH CENTURY: A TYPE STILL TO BE FOUND AT
COUNTRY AUCTIONS.

a fit, but two corners were easily opened, and the pieces were sawed in a mitre-box (no home is complete without one!), and then the size was right. The glass was missing, but the painting required none, and the frame and picture now look as if one was made for the other.

Auctions, though fascinating, are great time consumers, and we tell of experiences scattered over years of collecting.

Once in a while, at a city auction, the sale lags late, the afternoon is drowsy, the auctioneer and the thinning throng become indifferent, and there are then, sometimes, wonderful things to be had; as, one afternoon, six fine blue plates, much prized, that came to us for ten cents apiece. Maupassant, in one of his stories, describes such a sale, when the auction rooms seemed asleep and the auctioneer was listlessly knocking things down to listless bidders, whereupon a beautiful silk vestment of the Louis XV period was sold, which, used later to cover a Louis XV chair, brought about the discovery in the lining of a faded old letter, which makes the story.

Perhaps the most amazing of all auctions was one, not fictional but actual, in France, the auction at which, under the rule of the Revolutionists, large part of the belongings of Versailles was sold. Three years before, nothing could have been more unthinkable. As well, nowadays, one might fancy selling at auction the contents of the British Museum!

Perhaps the most dramatic and unexpected of American auctions was that of over a century and a half ago, when the belongings of Sir Danvers Osborne were sold. Appointed Governor of New York, by the King, he arrived in New York City in 1753, with his household furniture, looking forward to a career of political and social distinction—but hanged himself within five days of his landing, on account of private griefs and threatened public troubles!   It is recorded that there were fine and splendid pieces auctioned at the sale; and how interesting it would be to know what has become of them!   For doubtless some of them are still in existence; splendid secretaries, Chippendale chairs, bandy-leg tables; the best obtainable of that excellent age.

What is said to have been the very first auction in England (for although auctions were an old Roman institution there followed a long period in which they seem to have been forgotten), was the sale of goods belonging to another English governor, on his return to England from the region which he had been governing; a governor, this, who holds a far greater degree of interest for Americans than did ever that unfortunate Osborne, although Osborne was English governor of New York and the other was an English governor of the East Indies—for this East Indian governor, the sale of whose goods on his return from India marked the beginning of a long, long line of delightful auctions, had been born in America, and although he had left this side of the Atlantic when ten years old and although he never came back, his career keeping him in England and in India instead, he never forgot Connecticut and New Haven, and forty or fifty years after he had left America he made a gift of some twenty-five hundred dollars and some books to a certain college over here, which on account of this generous patronage assumed his name—which was Yale! Never, surely, did so great and durable a nomenclatured fame come from a gift of such proportions!

At an auction, as anywhere else, although the collector may be amused or gratified or interested, to get something at a low price, he should always be ready to pay a good price rather than lose a prize. The important thing is, to get the desired piece into your possession; in that lies the best satisfaction of all; the matter of cost, interesting though it may be, is always secondary except when a too-high range of prices bars you from something you really wish for.

A very well-known auctioneer of fine collections of old things in New York, a shrewd observer of human nature, used to say that it was a better business investment for him to let a woman get a thing at a very great bargain, than to let a man have it, "for a woman will go and tell all her friends, and tell where she got it, and they will all come next day, but a man, getting something at a wonderfully low price, although he will tell of it, won't tell where he got it."

To ourselves, auctions mean rather a delightful expedition into the country, rather than the auction of the city, for always there is at least the country drive or motor run, and the charm of sky and roadside and hills. One does not love auctions for the auctions' sake alone but for the incidental pleasures and experiences, and it is well this is so, for not always does the auction yield a prize. We remember one delightful day, when, with some friends, we came unexpectedly upon a road marked "Old China Road"—such a delightful name and so full of delightful suggestion!—and we at once explored the road; what collector so dead to romance as not to do so! And we found an old and tumble-down house tucked away among trees beside a river's edge, an old house absolutely without a single antique in it from garret to cellar but with the dual traditions hovering vaguely about it that it had either been the home of a captain who had traded to China in the old sailing vessel days or else that it had been the home of a china collector of long ago; and, somehow, the very vagueness of it, the optional alternative of choice, had in itself something of allurement, and the finding of the strangely named road and of the old house with its fluted wainscot and great oval dining room, at the end of it, beside the water, was an experience full of interest; but no antique was to be found, and we turned back again, and in a little while found ourselves approaching another old house, with the road and the yard in front

of it crowded with fully fifty wagons, with a sprinkling
of carriages and a dozen or so automobiles; and the
gathering was for an auction and in five or ten minutes
it was to begin. We thought ourselves in the greatest
luck. How could it be otherwise!

But it took only a few minutes' brief reconnaissance
to find that there was not a single thing that even in
the remotest degree resembled a desirable antique.
The ancient house, the old neighbourhood, the throng of
people, meant nothing but a social coming together
of friendly folk.

As a social country gathering, indeed, the country
auction holds high place. The auctioneer is usually
clever, with a fund of humour that appeals to his audience. There is persiflage, there is friendliness, there is
greeting of acquaintances. And country auctioneers
are themselves an interesting class, and with odd local
differences, as, that those of Eastern Pennsylvania always wear gloves at a sale. Country auctions are usually held either in early spring or late fall, at the changing of the seasons, and the idea of buying old treasure
set out under the apple blossoms, or in an autumn garden, in the mild air, in the shadow of an old homestead,
has an appeal to any lover of the old.

English auctions and auctioneers are not so interesting; judging from a description by Thackeray, in which
he pictures an auctioneer as sitting on a great mahogany dining table, employing all the artifices of

eloquence, enthusiasm, entreaty, reason and despair, imploring, commanding, roaring, bellowing. Assuredly not an agreeable description; Americans would not patiently remain through such a sale.

Vendues, as country sales are often called, do not yield the things you want quite so often as they did a few years ago, for sales in the country are now more likely to attract professional dealers. After the first year of collecting, one pays less attention to auctions except when they are near home or are come upon by some felicitous chance or at some special place where the sale is sure to have something worth while; and always, whether in city or country, if there is a chance to walk through the rooms and glance about, the experienced collector can tell in that brief survey whether or not there are things worth waiting for.

At a country auction it is always well to look just outside of the kitchen door, under the little porch, for there is likely to be something there that has been forgotten—the "hired-man's" looking glass, which, become shabby, has descended from indoor use to outer banishment. At three separate country sales we have found, at the kitchen door, forgotten and left hanging there, really excellent old mirror frames that needed only restoration. Just take the mirror off the nail and hand it to the auctioneer and for almost nothing your treasure trove is yours.

At a large sale of old-time character in the country

the early hours are occupied with selling the things at the barn and in the dooryard, out by the peonies and the box-bushes, and under the dooryard fruit trees; hay and horses and harness, and hoes and ropes and tools and the grindstone and then the churns and the milk-pans, the benches, settees and wooden chairs; and only after all this does the auctioneer lead the way through room after room, selling things in each, with as many people as possible wedging and crowding along, or he stands at the front door or on the edge of the porch and has things handed out and held up in view beside him. And always there is the accompanying and continuous crackle of peanuts; a sale in the country seems always to produce a peanut vender and the crackle and crack go on through the whole sale.

A village sale at which a bid of twenty-five cents secured a really good and picturesque four-poster bed is among our pleasantest recollections. Four-posters are nearly always sold for quite small prices, and the reason seems to be that they give an impression of taking up altogether too much room, although there is really no reason why a four-poster should take up any more room than an ordinary bed, except as to its up-and-down dimensions. Yet it is not only the buyer of to-day who feels that they are large, for it seems as if they have always given that impression. Dickens somewhere describes a despotic monster of a four-post bedstead, straddling over the whole room, putting one of his legs into the fireplace, and another into the doorway, and squeezing the little washstand into its corner. But in any room, except for height, a four-poster really fits just as easily as any other kind; indeed, they are outfitted with the same size of mattress as ordinary-size beds, which quite settles the question of their own size.

We remember an auction at a long, old stone house; a house that seemed full of time and all the mystery of time; a house that did not face the road, did not seem to pay any attention to the road, but faced away from it toward the southward, over a lush green meadow and a spring that gurgled away from an ancient springhouse shaded by two enormous sycamores. It was the house of an early Pennsylvania family, and the early Pennsylvania homesteads were always near a springhouse above a spring.

It was an auction at which we were not in the end disappointed although at the first we were quite thoroughly so. For although there were a number of things that were worth while, such as an old desk and some tables, they were of such kinds as we already possessed; and so although they sold at moderate prices they did not tempt us. But there was one thing we really did want, a highboy, of particularly good shape, and we bid well for it but before long saw that the price was mounting and mounting—we learned afterwards that the dealer who finally acquired it had a commission from one of his customers to get such a highboy even at a very high price. And so the auction yielded us nothing at all, although we had seen a mahogany desk with a good secret drawer sell for eight dollars; for we had been determined to hold back on any ordinary tempting purchase so as to get the highboy.

But there was an aftermath and a most charming one. For it was spring time, and all over the meadow were patches of bright green which, examined, proved to be bunches of daffodils, in tight and root-bound masses, pushing their way up through the ground in the promise of their yellow glory soon to come. For generations these daffodils had grown here, massing thicker and thicker year by year.

And we forgot the disappointing sale and told the old father (he was going to the far-distant Pacific coast with the younger generation) that we should like to buy some of the daffodils and his sad old eyes brightened with happiness. He told us he could remember his mother and his grandmother picking them in that meadow in the spring and that they had been brought from England and planted in that meadow by the bride of the man who had built the house. He was glad that some one should care for the old flowers and helped us to find a spade and dig them up. He then wanted to refuse the money, but his sidelong glance at the daughter-in-law spoke what was in his mind, and he feared to venture. And even the daughter-in-law was graciously pleased to be gratified, and so we went away in a sort of atmosphere of happiness, and that very day the daffodils were planted at our own home, the bulbs being carefully disentangled to give room for flowering and growth, and that very year they bloomed in their sweet yellow glow for us, and for several years, since then, they have most pleasantly lined the path leading from our library door.

At an auction on a bleak March day, where some sixty or seventy people were crowded into a spacious kitchen, the biggest room in the house, with the auctioneer enthroned upon a wooden chair in the middle and a great stove sending out its heat at one side, suddenly there came an ominous cracking sound and a wild rush to get out, with cries of, "The floor's going down!" And miraculously no one was hurt in the scramble, and in a few minutes faces were massed at the windows and the doors but no one dared to enter, and there, still enthroned on his chair, was the auctioneer, the only one who had not fled! And he looked placidly about and said: "This is nothing! Why, twice I have gone right through to the cellar with all the folks! Now, the next lot—" And on he went, with perfect and enviable calm. And the bidding went on again, too, but mainly through the windows, and the crowd became keenly diverted by a contest between an elderly husband and his wife for six jars of thin and mysterious pickles which both of them took to be jam; and the two could not see each other and so neither of them knew that they were rivals in bidding, although everybody else quickly knew for the word was whispered rapidly around. And the husband got the pickles.

When the auction was over, and all who could find a seat or a footing had piled aboard of a big suburban trolley car, all in high and gleeful spirits, it was funny to see two well-dressed women, each with a huge mirror on her lap and desperately frightened lest an accident occur but each triumphant, and to see a dignified doctor on the front platform balanced upon a seatless chair that he had bought, and to see a woman holding a big blue washbowl and pitcher—there is never any wrapping paper at a country auction—and to see other men and women with chairs and little tables that were packed straddlingly in the aisle as if to trip the conductor. And then, in a momentary silence, a silence which in an instant became complete, for every one listened, there came the growling voice of the husband who had bid against his wife for the supposed jam which he had now, on opening a jar, found to be pickles, and the two went on in angry antiphony, one growling and the other shrill, to a delighted audience.

"It was you!"

"It was you!"

"It was you and the stuff's only pickles!"

"It was you ran it up and you thought it was jam!"

"We came all this way to begin a collection—"
"And you made me buy pickles instead—"
"We were going to get genuine antiques—"
"And it's pickles and not even jam!"

CHAPTER XVI

IF an English collector is asked in regard to old glass he will reply, with amusingly characteristic intolerance, that it is of two kinds: the good old glass, made in England, and the bad old glass, made in the Low Countries.

That England made any of the poorer glass is to an Englishman quite inconceivable, and if you seek to make him believe it by examples he will declare that the examples are not of English make; that they are either foreign or fraudulent. The famous Irish glass made at Waterford, he includes under his flag. As to American make, he will not admit that there was any of that kind of old glass. And in all this he will be so absolutely honest and sincere that you need thoroughly to know your own ground if you wish to remain standing upon it.

Glass making is an industry dating back to remote antiquity, and in modern times the various countries of Europe made excellent glass, the Venetians being the most noted for it, and England taking up the manufacture with Venetian workmen in Elizabeth's time and more actively in the days of Charles the First. Such of the old glass now obtainable in America as was not made on this side of the ocean is principally English, German and Dutch; there are quantities of the Bohemian glass of the mid-nineteenth century, but this last is seldom a matter of collection. America began very early to make glass; the manufacture was attempted at the early and unfortunate settlement of Jamestown, and after that, in the next century, in a number of places, and it was made in very delightful and original forms, so that it may well be a source of pride to an American, this glass of early American make. This was notably so with the glass made by the picturesque and famous Baron Stiegel, in the years immediately before the Revolution.

The attention of most collectors has not yet been turned toward glass, and this is largely because most of it, being unmarked, is a little difficult to classify. But it offers a delightful field for American collecting.

Cup-plates, a few years ago, rose to a high range of prices, for such simple things; but they are still findable for the hunting; cup-plates, whether of glass or china, being the little plates, three-and-a-half or four inches in diameter, upon which, along in the early years of the 1800's, our forefathers set their teacups or coffeecups when they drank, for they drank out of their saucers. Saucer drinking was quite good form, as we remember a very precise old gentleman telling us, when he was looking at some of our cup-plates. Large quantities of cup-plates, in glass, were made in Sandwich, Massachusetts, and in the early New Jersey glass factories. They are of pressed glass, made by a plunger, and the designs have simple attractiveness and many are of patriotic kind, like those of "Bunker Hill, 1775"; although this date should not be associated with the manufacture of the cup-plate for the monument on the hill fixes the date of its making.

Glass was made at Manheim, in Lancaster County, Pennsylvania, by Baron Stiegel, who used to travel in great state, with coach and eight horses, and was accustomed to have himself welcomed home after an absence by a great orchestra assembled on the roof of his big house; he made large quantities of an excellent kind of glass, much of it for shipment to what were then distant points, such as New York City—and that was certainly distant from an interior Pennsylvania county, for so fragile a thing as glass, in the old-time days of bad roads and sailing ships.

The Stiegel glass has rather arbitrarily come into great demand among collectors; it is excellent glass in quaint shapes and is pre-Revolutionary in make; it is one of the earliest Colonial products on which enthusiasm can be lavished, but nothing essentially remarkable; but after all, the picturesque personality of the Baron is sufficient to give his glass an extra price and vogue over the products of the little village of Sandwich out on Cape Cod and little glass factories in Jersey without aristocratic sponsors. There is a great deal in a name, and a coach and eight horses made an impression then and do so now. The authenticity of his ware needs to be carefully looked into, for much is called his without certainty.

Our best specimen of Stiegel glass was obtained from an old house within a half mile of the Stiegel glass factory, now vanished; it is a fine "flip" glass, six inches high, has a hollow folded rim, and a roughly broken pontil mark upon the bottom, and rings, when struck, with the clear tone of a bell.

Stiegel glass may be described as graceful in shape, very resonant—remarkably so, indeed—always with a pontil mark on the bottom, and made in clear glass, slightly blackish in the thick spots, and also in blue and mulberry colours. The forms are quaint. In the last year of the factory painted glass was made, for all this glass was made by German-Americans and Germans have always liked painted glass.

The best way and in fact the only way to learn old glass is to study its possibilities in museums and private collections, and gradually there comes the intuitive judging as to looks and ring that differentiates the old from the new or the imitation.

In some degree, the pontil mark is the best clue—the rough spot left by the workman's blow-rod in the early days of glass making; for in old pieces it is to be found on the bottom of each piece; and then came the period of, say, about 1800, when this rough spot was ground

THE POSSIBILITIES OF PEWTER: ILLUSTRATING MANY OF THE VARIED
AND INTERESTING EXAMPLES STILL TO BE FOUND, IN THIS BEAU-
TIFUL OLD WARE.

SUGGESTIONS IN OLD THINGS OF
BRASS: OPEN-WORK FENDER,
WITH ANDIRONS, SHOVEL,
TONGS AND POKER; WARMING-PANS, AND OLD KETTLES; THE
CENTER ONE HAMMERED, THE OTHER SPUN.

smooth, and then the period when, through change in methods of making, there was no mark at all on the bottom.

Glass bottles with patriotic devices were commonly made in early days in America. They have a sort of greenish cast, and are attractive, with their oval shapes and smooth and lipless necks; attractive, as well as highly interesting. Washington, Kossuth, favourite frigates, and, of a later date, Zachary Taylor—such as these can still be found, blown in the bottles from moulds, and are so thoroughly American in make and character as to be well worth while.

But before very long the glass collector becomes more ambitious, and is not satisfied without specimens of excellent make, and then comes the search for really beautiful decanters and for wine glasses with baluster stems, and air bubbles called "tears" in the stem, and the rare old engraved glasses and those with white twists and spirals in their stems, and the large cut or blown glass jugs of the eighteenth or early nineteenth century. Most of these kinds that are to be found in America were made in England or the Netherlands.

And it is astonishing how much is still to be found in this ware so easily broken. We ourselves have been so fortunate as to gather in two large glass jugs of veritable old-time make, one thirteen inches high, and the other much shorter, but measuring eight inches across, from end of handle to tip of lip, this one being of heavy "rock crystal" as the finest old English glass is called, cut in old cuttings and of extreme weight. Our most precious possession, in glass, is a wine-jug, simple and shapely, blown, and then both cut on a wheel and etched. This is of Venetian make and of the seventeenth century.

Of wine glasses and liqueur glasses we have found quite a number, one or two or three at a time, and most of them not far from home. One set of old wine glasses, cut closely in fine line cuts at the bottom of the bowl, was the possession of an old American family in Connecticut for one hundred years.

Of early silver there is not so much to find easily nowadays, and that little is seldom to be obtained for little cost; but silver is a thing that comes to collectors frequently by inheritance, for "old family silver" has such an impressive phrase that old silver is handed down where antiques of other kinds have been thrown aside. We have two beautiful little toddy ladles, and have found several sets of thin old spoons, especially some of excellent odd shape, slender, with very pointed handles, of the late eighteenth century, and we have some old three-legged salts that came by inheritance.

But family silver can give heartaches to a collector, and we know of two odd cases of aunts and nephews and tankards. One family had a very old silver tankard of Dutch origin, associated with the founder of the family in New York, and two aunts, its possessors, wishing to please a favourite nephew, said that they were going to give it to him. He was so happy that he told all his friends, but became a little worried when told that it was at a silversmith's, and he wondered why it was there, but could only wait. And at length it came. And it had been melted and made into an ice-pitcher! The aunts had thought the old tankard was a little too shabby for their much-loved nephew! The other case was also that of a tankard, hall-marked 1720, and of known descent through seven generations. The aunties—another set of aunties—this time also gave it to a silversmith, and he covered one side with a 1913 inscription as if it were a last year's yacht trophy!

Both of these "improvements" were made under instructions, but even the best of silversmiths need to be forewarned lest they change without instructions, as in a recent case in which, given a wonderful old American silver teapot to repair, which had its eagle spout a little worn, the silversmith actually cut off the eagle's head and rounded the spout into a neat little tidy ending!

Buying old silver is a very different matter from buying old furniture, for silver can seldom be bought to advantage from the individual owner, who is almost certain to have an exaggerated notion of value; not a fair or commensurate idea, but one that sets the value far beyond the prices of the same things in the shops. Of the simple forms of old silver there is no shortage; and in the large cities there is a source, open to collectors, which can be followed up with excellent advantage, for there are little shops and working jewellers that advertise the buying of old gold and silver, and there cannot be so much buying without selling, and on investigation you will find that the little shops take in very considerable quantities, the destination of which is the melting-pot except for old shapes that are recognized and rescued. We know of more than one collector who has arranged for a standing option with several buyers and smelters, for what they take in of certain kinds of old silver, and, although one of these is in a city a good many hundred miles inland, there are admirable results. But old silver is not obtainable by the basketful in one visit; there must be years of patience and purchase.

Thieves, of course, are frequently selling old silver, and the collector who buys silver which he suspects has been stolen is at least saving it from being melted up. Ash-cart men and janitors gather in a good deal of silver; new mostly, but old, too, and sell it to the silver buyers. It is amazing, how much silver, with a large proportion of old silver (for people who possess old spoons and forks like to use them), is thrown out with melon rinds and grape fruit and lettuce leaves; it is amazing how much is carelessly dropped into the waste and thrown away. That old spoons are often very light in weight adds easily to this possibility.

A curious case was that of a neighbour of ours in a New York apartment house years ago. She was giving a dinner and looked about for a dozen old and valued spoons of her husband's family, marked with a name spelled in a peculiar way. But only three of the spoons were to be found.

But the janitor's wife, who was hired on special occasions to assist the cook, hearing mention of old spoons not being found, said:

"Mrs. D., I have some old spoons, quite old-fashioned. Perhaps they would help you out for to-night."

And she went downstairs and came back with a whole handful—of varying interest—and among them were nine marked with the peculiarly spelled family name.

"Wherever did you find these spoons?" she was asked.

"Just like the others—lots of them come down the dumbwaiter in the trash." It was all so matter of course, and it was so evident that they had not been stolen, and that she had no idea to whom they belonged in that findings-is-keepings bottom of the dumbwaiter, and it was so clear that they had been carelessly dropped into the daily debris, that our friend merely bought back the family spoons and thought it best not to explain. Here were the precious lost spoons; that was the main thing; and she keeps them in the safety deposit box now!

There used to be, in the long ago, immense quantities of silver used even for such things as table-tops and similar furnishings, in the days when kings lived like kings, but most of that silver has been melted down, and largely in times of war. Books of travel, and memoirs, have descriptions of great variety of silver furnishings, but such things are not often to be found to-day even in museums.   It will be remembered that the andirons in Imogen's bedroom were two Cupids made of silver.

In Sheffield plate, which is silver on copper, there are splendid opportunities and possibilities in tea-urns and salvers, and open-work sugar-baskets, and we ourselves have been able to find such things as candlesticks, some really beautiful ones for extremely reasonable sums, and we have also a couple of bottle-stands; "coasters" as they are called, of ancient make, on mahogany bottoms, which were given to us by their long-time possessors.   They were in so sad a state of dilapidation as to demand re-plating, for there was more copper showing than silver! Replating cannot be done by the old Sheffield process, which was a process by which the silver was applied before the silver was even rolled into thin form for shaping into its final form, and is a process out of use anyway. And after all, the coasters still have age and association and beauty of shape and design, and anything that possesses such claims to distinction is well worth while.

With articles of Sheffield plate, all decorations in relief, such as beadings and gadroons, leaves and borders, are of solid silver, and we have at one time or another met several owners of very much worn pieces who firmly believe that they possess articles of copper with silver trimmings!—the explanation being that in the course of decades of use and polishing the plating was entirely worn off the copper, while the silver of course remained silver.

Every collector gathers old brass, for it comes naturally and inevitably, in varied shapes; and andirons, of course, and kettles for actual use as in past days, and candlesticks, which look so delightfully old-fashioned and utilitarian and so exactly fit the landscape, so to speak, and which may also still be handily used even in these days of modern lighting. Looks alone would be sufficient, for old brass, to justify gathering it, but it always adds a fine touch of interest to put old things to actual use as well—although there are uses and uses—as, the couple told of in Barnaby Rudge, who made a habit of using brass candlesticks to throw at each other.

If the process of making some of these old things is understood it gives an added interest in the collecting of them. Such brasses as old candlesticks and andirons are hollow cast, then turned to a smooth surface on a lathe, and burnished. Kettles are either hammered, or spun from sheet metal. If hammered, the surface shows innumerable round spots, all so smooth as scarcely to be seen. Bottoms are oftentimes dovetailed in.

"Spun" brass does not mean that brass threads were used! Far from it. It means that brass, rolled thin, sheet brass, was held against a wooden mould and by the pressure of smooth tools was rounded into shape while mould and brass were spinning round at great speed. The process of spinning cannot make the entire globe of a kettle in one process; a kettle or other globe-shaped piece, if spun, must be made in two separate pieces, hemispheres, which are then brazed together, and there is a fine little line to be seen, on close examination, marking where the brazing has been done. Finding this line, or else the hammer marks, is the way to tell how a kettle has been made. The modern process of making brass articles by stamping out sheets of it is altogether apart from any possible interest for a collector.

It is one of the pleasantest experiences of collecting, this natural and gradual development of side lines, such as glass and silver and brass. Iron, too, is another line that yields great pleasure, not alone for its minor possibilities in quaint, hand-made simple utensils, but for important furnishings, such as andirons. As a general thing, andirons that are very much worth while are not iron at all, contradictory though it may seem, but brass; but there are some exceptions, as, the rare and much-sought-for Hessian andirons, the jaunty-stepping sturdy little Hessian soldiers, made, so old tradition tells, of captured cannon; and the so-called George Washington andirons, which are still rarer—a pair of iron Washingtons facing out with stately dignity into the room—perhaps, in this case, with some patriotic idea of being guardian of our American hearthstones. But it must be admitted that these andiron Washingtons look more like some British admiral than they do like the President.

SIMPLE, PRESENT-DAY POSSIBILITIES IN OLD SHEFFIELD-PLATE; COF-
FEE-URN, CANDLESTICKS, COASTERS, AND THREE-LEGGED SALTS.
SLENDER OLD SILVER SPOONS, WITH SILVER TODDY-LADLES, PEPPERS
AND SUGAR-BASIN.

1 OLD WINE-GLASSES, WITH THE LARGE BARON STIEGEL GLASS BESIDE THE GLASS CUP-PLATES AT THE RIGHT.

2 A JUG OF ROCK CRYSTAL; TALL BLOWN JUG; FINE CUT DECANTER, 18TH CENTURY; WINE JUG, VENETIAN, 17TH CENTURY; EARLY AMERICAN DECANTER BLOWN IN A MOLD; EXQUISITE CUT-GLASS BOTTLE, ONE OF A SET OF SIX.

3 IN THE CENTER, A PORTUGUESE WINE BOTTLE; ON EITHER SIDE, EARLY AMERICAN BOTTLES.

Most interesting of all such side lines is the collecting of pewter: for there are such delightfully varied shapes of this material, and it is still to be found at not too prohibitive prices. The possibilities in pewter are very great.

It is an attractive ware, but its beauty is quite independent of large intrinsic value, as with gold and silver, and is also independent of any beauty of cutting or hammering. It is the glow of pewter, its soft dulness of colour, its lines and proportion, and its fine simplicity, that are its charm.

Most of the pewter to be found in America is of English or German make, but some has American marks, such as an eagle and "New York." Much of it is marked, with stampings, and a great deal may be made out from these marks, even though many of them are almost illegible, and although the marks were never, as was the case with the marks on silver, matter of strict government regulation. It is worth remembering, too, that silver marks are "hall-marks," from the records of Goldsmiths' Hall, in London (which included silver as well as gold), and that the marks or punchings on pewter are "touch marks." Hall-marks on silver tell the town in which the article is manufactured and the year of manufacture by means of the differently lettered alphabets, changed at regular periods by the goldsmiths; and if the sovereign's head occurs it means that a stamp act was laid upon silver at that time, and that it paid a duty to the Crown.

The basis of pewter is tin. Pewter can be made without lead but not without tin. Fine pewter was made from tin and brass. Brittleness was a property to be avoided in pewter and a surface that took a fine polish was desired, hence other substances were also used, such as antimony and bismuth. Pewter with a large proportion of lead is easily picked out; it is leady in looks and when shined soon loses its silvery lustre and relapses into a dull surface. Some pewter plates are so fine as to stack together so neatly and trimly that six are but an inch through. There are astonishing differences in the weight of pewter, some being very heavy and some light.

Pewter, more than almost anything else, was connected in an intimate way with the daily life of the past; or at least, to those who gather pewter, it somehow gives that impression. It is a very old material, having been used for many centuries and by many nations. When England raised the immense ransom to save Richard Cœur de Lion from his captivity, it demanded such an immense melting down of vessels of silver and gold throughout the length and breadth of the land that the use of pewter was again permitted in the churches, though it had long been forbidden as being too cheap a material for churchly use.

There are many who think of pewter in terms of plates alone, or at the most in terms of plates and tank-

ards: and plates and tankards—especially tankards!—
are highly attractive; the tankards, especially, because
their varied shapes point out different countries; as, the
typical German, the typical English, the Dutch, the
Norman—thus giving to collecting an additional tang.
And the pleasure of pewter collecting is greatly increased when one begins to realise what a wide variety
of articles there is besides plates and tankards; our own
gathering has such unusual things in pewter as a lamp,
a sugar bowl, a spice-dish delightfully tooled, a tall
flagon, cups, pepper-shakers and jugs. And this list
is suggestive only, and not in any sense meant to cover
collecting possibilities in pewter. Our pewter flagon
is eleven inches high, and was made in New York and
contrasts oddly with a tiny measure of English make,
which is only an inch and three-quarters in height and
bears twelve excise marks, suggestive of the days when
Robert Burns was an excise man and went about putting marks on pewter measures.

Although some of our pewter has been picked up in
distant and widely apart places, it need not be thought
that one need necessarily go far from home to get attractive examples, for in a town less than two miles from
our home we obtained one of our best pewter tankards.
A woman, one of a family who trace back to an ancestor
who received his lands by deed in the time of William
Penn, had for thirty years had her morning milk left at
her door in this tankard. "Its cover kept out flies," she

said simply. But in course of time there came the modern idea of delivery in individual bottles, and this tankard, rather battered from years of front-step use, was relegated to a top pantry shelf and forgotten. It is a recent acquisition of ours, and came to us for just one dollar; this being mentioned, as to local finding and reasonable price, to give encouragement to those who doubt the possibilities of to-day. But one should not hesitate to pay well for pewter, for the supply is gradually on the wane.

The necessary polishing of pewter is dreaded by some, but it need not be taken very seriously. For table use it may have needed very great care, but for a collection, washing with hot water and soap and a slight polishing once a year keeps it in a good condition, half way between brilliance and dulness.

But we have two pieces which no polishing will help —shapely, both of them, and more recently acquired than the tankard for milk, and from a house on the same street, these two pieces being a huge tankard, called by its owner an ewer, and a deep basin that goes with it. These two old pieces are of old and admirable make, but are entirely covered with gold paint, having been selected for ornament by whoever owned them in that curious era in taste when all sorts of homely household articles were painted or decorated: the well-remembered era of the decorated fireshovel.

And thus far, we have been unable to take off the

offending gilt! Banana oil, benzine, lye, hot water, kerosene—we have not found the proper solvent; but we shall, and in any case this pewter is one of the many examples of admirable and possible present-day finds.

CHAPTER XVII

SO very many old-time things have to be bought in a somewhat broken-down condition or not at all, that the collector ceases to look upon this as a disadvantage; he says to himself that he is fortunate in finding a broken specimen; he is fortunate in getting it before it had been broken into entire uselessness; and fortunate that its condition has made the owner glad to sell. And it is only through personal experience that any one may come to know whether or not a piece of old furniture is too badly broken to deserve repairing, this being dependent not only upon the kind of wear and tear and the prospective cost of restoration but also upon the value of the article when restored.

But from the first the collector realises that there is no intrinsic benefit in a condition of wreckage, that a broken leg is no advantage, that wormholes are not precious assets, that a bulged top is not in itself a good thing, that an antique clean and sound and unbroken is in itself better than an antique dirty and smashed and rickety. But he also comes to realise that indirectly there may be and usually are positive advantages in finding articles in rather bad condition; that breakages

AN EIGHTEENTH CENTURY CLOCK, AN EMPIRE MIRROR AND A WASH-
STAND, ALL RESTORED; A LOWBOY, RESTORED FROM A CONDITION
OF SHAKING WRECKAGE; AND LADDER-BACK CHIPPENDALES, RE-
STORED, AND EXTREMELY WELL WORTH IT.

A SEATLESS CHAIR AND A RUSH-SEAT, AWAITING RESTORATION; AND A BANDY-LEG TABLE OF ABOUT 1740; A WRECK, AWAITING RESTORATION AND WELL WORTH IT.

cents, and of how Clemina answered, so softly and gently: "We women could buy things, too, but it is pleasant to do things with our own hands."

There is a primitive school of repairing that does not repair; as, when an old tip-table becomes out of order, and the countryman who owns it just drives a couple of tenpenny nails through it to set it right and then gives it a tasty coat of green paint and sets it out on the porch with a flowerpot on it.

A friend bought for only four dollars a veneered and exquisitely inlaid lowboy, which had once been a positive beauty, but it had been kept for a long time in a damp place and the veneer and inlay were actually loose and flaking off. We were with her when she bought it, and realised what a prize had been found, but she told us afterwards that her husband had made her feel blue by saying that it would cost too much to repair. She sent for a restorer, and asked him how expensive it would be to put it in order, whereupon he said—for he had gathered from her tone that it was a case of disappointment—"I'll take it off your hands for twenty-five dollars just as it stands." Naturally, then, she had it repaired and prizes it most highly. The veneer and inlay had to be cleaned and reset—a small task compared with replacing bruised or missing parts.

Veneer, when not too badly broken, is one of the things that can be repaired at home; veneer can be bought in sheets, and we remember a place far over on the East

Side, in New York, where it can be procured. One sheet will mend a whole collection of small nicks and missing fragments and lasts for years. Broken lines of inlay can be reset, with holly or satinwood, or holly blackened for ebony mends, without the trouble of sending your old piece away. Often, sending an old piece of furniture by express entails more serious injury than the one that was to be repaired. And as to little breaks, they can often be mended by some such contrivance as boring a hole and inserting a skewer of wood. Two of such skewers and some good glue will hold a shattered piece together, or hold down a splinter, better than nails. The home mender, indeed, too often reaches for a hammer and nails and fears to try a glue-pot! Yet it is surprising how much can be done with good glue. A baking powder tin and a mucilage brush make a good outfit, for glueing, and it is better to buy good glue than to bother about getting a real glue-pot! Good glue comes in little sheets and is translucent and should be freshly made for each using. A set of wooden clamps to hold the mend in a firm grip until set will repay many times over for its purchase.

But, of course, for extensive repairs, it is better to send to an old-furniture repairer; only, it is not always easy to find a really good one, whose place is within reasonable distance.

Articles too badly broken should be left unbought. The other day we saw, thrown into a corner outside an up-country cross-roads store, a huge Windsor chair that had once been unusually fine but which had lost two legs and the upper part of its extension back. Mutilated Windsors are a temptation, and coming upon it unexpectedly made us feel particularly disposed to take it along, and this desire was deepened by the wish to save it—every collector will know what we mean; the pathetic appeal of a broken antique, for rescue—but we let it go, for it was really wrecked past even an enthusiast's desire to restore. But the beginner should learn not lightly to deem a case hopeless; for many a thing passed by as irreparable by the inexperienced is really capable of beautiful and easy restoration. The motto of the enthusiast is "Never too late to mend!"

Warped table tops can be straightened, and dents can be raised, and lost handles can be replaced, and a host of things can be done.

Finding mahogany painted into ugliness has often checked a collector's ambition to possess, but it should never do so, for paint can be removed by scraping, and a desperately bad looking case, though discouraging to the inexperienced, is really no worse than one that is just ordinarily bad looking, as, some article that has an old coat of varnish; for it all scrapes the same and with the same amount of work. But if the wood is dyed instead of painted, or if it is scorched by heat, it is very difficult, it is well-nigh impossible, to renovate except by the plane.

Old mirrors can often be delightfully restored, for broken or shabby frames can readily be mended or regilded. It is peculiarly interesting to restore an old mirror, for it always seems to be holding the long, long past in its depths. Nathaniel Hawthorne used to feel deeply the mystery of old mirrors and loved to write of it. If the glass of an old mirror has clouded or is marred it is possible to have it resilvered, but it is better to leave it with its dull-blue, or if it is really too bad for that, it is better to have a new glass in the old-time frame. Five times, in all, we have tried resilvering with varying degrees of failure, and never with really excellent results.

With some kinds of old-fashioned furniture, and especially the old Dutch marquetry, it is not alone a matter of getting it into good condition but of keeping it in good condition, especially in the dry heat of most American homes. It was a wealthy American collector who, afflicted with expensive French furniture that would keep getting shaky in the heat of his big city home, said, upon being told that the French monarchs kept quarters in their palaces for a head cabinet-maker for keeping the furniture in order, that he could quite understand it; in fact it was about the most sensible thing he had ever heard about any royal Louis; for he himself surely needed a resident repairer, right there in his New York house, so that, as he expressed it, he could be sure of sitting on his chairs and sofas without fear and trembling—fear on his part and trembling on the part of the furniture.

We have personally had such fortunate and satisfactory experiences in finding old-time specimens, wrecked and unwrecked, as to show how very many attractive possibilities there are. You merely need to look for them! It is vastly better, surely, to find a wrecked or damaged treasure and have it restored under your own supervision than to buy it already furbished and restored; in the first case, the piece becomes very intimately your own, and you know, what you can never know when an article has been carefully restored before you see it, precisely what has been done to it and that the original design has not been tampered with.

As encouragement in finding repairable wrecks we need not refer to our own experiences only but to those of any collectors who enthusiastically collect. And as example we shall quote from a letter recently received from one:

"Hearing there was to be a sale at a farmhouse south of Coatesville I walked out to the farm a few days before the sale to look at the things. A storm was coming up and I was anxious to get home but before I left some good spirit prompted me to look into the spring house and there I found a pie-crust table. I asked the old man what he would take for it and he said: 'What! That old flower stand! It's shaky, and just look at the flower-pot marks on it. The women folks had it on the

back porch for years. You can take it for a quarter!'
I did!" It is easy to imagine how the shakiness was
made firm and the flower-pot marks disappeared, on
this rarest of old tables to find.

The memory of various wrecks that we did not
repair comes as a keen regret: not regret for lost opportunity but regret that the pieces going to wreck were not
to be obtained. Some were in the possession of the
United States Government, which holds a very large
amount of fine old furniture that is neither valued nor
taken care of—neither is it given over to collectors who
would both care for it and value it. It is in old navy-
yard buildings, in marine hospitals, in old military and
naval homes. Quite a proportion of such buildings were
built in the early 1800's and furnished with excellent
mahogany of Empire and late Sheraton designs. This
old mahogany accorded beautifully with the great rooms,
the fine staircases and doors and windows, of the temple-
like architecture that was a typically national style, for
public buildings, a century ago.

Most of this fine old furniture, which, harboured in
public buildings, did not feel the iconoclastic storms of
the bad taste era, is still existent, but much of it is now
broken, and fallen from its high estate into back halls
and remote cellar-ways, growing constantly more dilapidated as age creeps on apace. The good taste of some
officer in charge, or his wife, may bring them out into
their own again, rubbed and polished and honoured, but

not often; they are shabby and the taste of most of those in charge banishes them to obscure places. There seems to be no way, even when they are discarded and dishonoured, in which they can pass into a private ownership that would give them care. They may be broken up or thrown away but not given away or sold or taken by the officers on leaving. One of our Presidents and his family were lovers of the old and did much to preserve the antiques of the White House and place them in proper setting—though many a First Lady of the Land has been a furniture Philistine!—and one wishes that they had also secured the care and restoration of furniture in public buildings of minor note.

Other places where we have seen wrecks dumbly begging for care are certain endowed schools. We know of two in particular, both of them endowed a century ago but so lightly endowed as now to be sorely straitened by the high cost of living. One of these schools, placed in large and spacious old grounds, occupies a great, half Gothic, dreary building much incommoded for lack of sufficient money to warm it, paint it, supply it with adequate plumbing. The little orphans sit and dangle their feet on old Heppelwhite sofas that are bruised, nicked and wearing out—the price of one would outfit a needed bathroom!—and little girls dust with housewifely care but children's fingers the prisms on an exquisite set of girandoles sadly in need of repair—never were there finer ones, and how collectors would strive for them!—and the children dine at old banqueting tables whose feet are tipped with brass, and there are splendid sideboards, all more or less in need of restoration; Sheraton in the halls and Empire in the dining-room; the one in the dining-room having four Egyptian caryatides, with bearded head and curiously stiff feet, across its front: and the little child who was acting as guide—a well-cared-for and cheerful and dear little girl—said: "I always think that is Abraham Lincoln on our sideboard!"—Well, she loved the old sideboard and her little brain was busy and she had wondered what the caryatides really meant, and that was more than some wiser, older and richer elders do.

All the personal and very exquisite possessions of the founder were left to this school, well-managed but with no permission to sell and with an income not sufficient to buy new things and save the old. And the huge silver vault, set into a stone wall, behind an iron door, is something never to be forgotten, for in it are pierced baskets and salvers and urns and candelabra—two wagonloads! How fascinating such a place would seem if it were come upon in a distant land!—and here it is near home.

The other endowed school that we have in mind has also wonderful treasure, for there are such things as a pie-crust table, and a tall old secretary with wonderfully beautiful interior and all are used in the daily life and work of the school; in heavy and hard use, too.

Perhaps the oddest case of a wreck that we know of

was one in which a great chest was deliberately broken
to secure it; one of the very early chests, with lifting lid
and single drawer below. We came upon a dealer whom
we know, contemplating it as a wreck, and he said, with a
rueful smile, that he had bought the great chest in a
garret where it had been used for blanket storage; he
had bought it of a man who had said: "Now, you understand that you are to see to moving it"; and he had
unsuspiciously agreed, and paid his money, only to find,
then, that the chest could not be moved downstairs or
out of the window without reducing its size with an
axe! The owner had had it put into the garret while
that part of the house was building, and actually before
the roof was on—"And so I had to knock it to pieces
to get it!"

CHAPTER XVIII

THE CHARM OF A FITTING FINISH

GEORGE WASHINGTON, who used to keep account of his expenditures to a penny, thereby leaving for posterity a wealth of intimate facts, was not in the least small in money affairs, but quite the contrary, and yet he disliked to find that any of his money had been apparently squandered, as when he set down, indignantly, that he found it hard to believe that six thousand twelve-penny nails had been used in the building of one corn-crib. But had Washington ever had an armchair upholstered, and finished with brass tacks, he would ever afterward have been quite ready to believe in any number of nails in something that was so much larger than a chair! We ourselves have had the experience of upholstering a big Heppelwhite fireside chair and it was simply amazing how many packages of brass tacks were required. The literal count of tacks would run far up in the hundreds.

He who sees personally to upholstering some sturdy old-fashioned piece of furniture comes to a great appreciation of the structure. With that Heppelwhite, it was surprising to see how skilfully and even how wonderfully the framework had been made, with openings for drawing the edges of the cloth through instead of leaving them to be in some way fastened on the outside.

Such a thing as the necessity for guimpe edging would have been deemed a final atrocity by any old-time maker. The upholstering of Chippendale chairs met such edge problems by having the chair seats made of a four-sided frame of finished wood rabbeted to hold an inset and movable centre which was to be lifted out for upholstering and laid in again. The wood thus cleverly takes the wear upon the edges. These are ideal seats, easily recovered and comfortable to sit upon. Heppelwhite chairs were upholstered by drawing the material over the frame of the seat and well underneath the chair, and were characteristically finished along the lower edge of the seat with rows of brass tacks arranged in symmetrical designs.

When old-time chairs are re-upholstered, the old methods should be carefully followed, instead of the modern method of hiding all difficulties under a line of ugly guimpe, which seems to be intended for the concealment of structural defects.

Our Empire sofa needed a re-upholstering and we wished to have it done in such a way as to display its lines to the very best advantage. It had met with several re-upholsterings in its career, and was built up altogether too high, and springs had made it almost mountainous, and it had thus suffered from two kinds of unfitting finish frequently given to fine old pieces.

The springs were particularly needless. Such old sofas, Empire, Sheraton, Heppelwhite, were not meant for springs. And when one thinks of it, a sofa without springs is just as comfortable as one that has them—they are not meant for sleeping on—and the lines, and therefore the general looks, are very much better. Many an old sofa and many an old chair has been distorted by springs and a high and ill-shaped re-upholstering.

The Empire sofa, like the fireside chair, showed fascinating secrets of construction when stripped, and there was the same kind of spaces left in the framework for the drawing through of the covering material, and the back itself was intended to be unscrewed for upholstering, and in being replaced, it solves the problem of how the backs of the arms should have their edges covered.

Originally such a sofa was upholstered, as to seat and back, with a good thick packing of hair, and nothing is better for the re-upholstering. The old-fashioned idea was to give a firm and fairly soft seat—something very different from bare boards but even more different from the high-billowing springs.

High springs, or high-piled seats, have spoiled many a fine old piece. A Chippendale chair of unusually beautiful proportions looked almost homely when we obtained it, not because, in that case, of springs, but because of the piling up of stratum upon stratum of cloth on the seat under the final cross-stitch cover.

Upholstering is only one of numerous points to be

considered in finishing old furniture and keeping it in the desired condition. For one's home, old furniture must be in good condition for proper use, and must not be ragged or broken, although for a museum or an historical collection a considerable degree of disrepair may be desirable, if suggestive of the original use and the original owner and the condition in which he left it. But however this point is settled, a glaring or new-looking finish never and nowhere has a place with old furniture.

Any mahogany coming down from a hundred years ago, unless under most ideal conditions, has a surface of old polish that has grown opaque. If it is a wax polish, there has become embodied in it grime from some period of neglect; if a French polish, it has grown opaque from a slight checkering and disintegration of the surface which makes it impossible to see clearly the beauty and colour of the wood beneath. A new surface is therefore required, and the first move is to choose the man who is to do it. To be able to talk to this restorer of surfaces and to judge of his work it is necessary for the owner himself to know what has to be done and what should not be done.

First, the old surface must be removed, for nothing will revive its transparency. There are many patent removers in liquid form, but there is nothing so good as scraping—scraping with a dull steel blade with the edge held in a straight line at right angles to the grain of the wood. The patent liquid removers reduce the old polish to a sort of molasses, which very easily leaves a cloud, a sort of smeary dulness like a film, over the wood and under the new polish. Also, any liquid liberally applied, and allowed to stand for the purpose of loosening old varnish, will do more than this, for it will be likely to seep through and soften the glue which holds inlay or veneer in place. It is unwise to use sandpaper or glass in the removal of surfaces, for they scratch. Lye is also an injurious remover for it darkens the wood. The knife blade, or a dull steel edge, is really the only thing to use, and the scraping should be with the long grain of the wood. It is slow work, but simple of accomplishment, and can be done at home, either by the owner or under his supervision.

As to the finish of old wood, there are three, even four possibilities. There is the wax polish, which demands a thorough rubbing twice a year as a minimum; and there is the French polish, which gives a lustrous, permanent finish, dust-resisting, and does not turn white when struck a blow. This is applied by hand rubbing from a wad through which the shellac-compounded French polish seeps while the workman rubs. It is dry as soon as applied. Being a hand process, it is slower than brush work but is worth while. And there is varnish, applied with a brush, coat over coat, with more or less time and energy spent on rubbing down between coats. This varnish process, and this only, is what the ordinary workman will give you. Its faults are that it fractures into white or yellowish marks if it is accidentally struck, and that it is usually too shiny, although it is possible to remedy this by a final rubbing down with rotten stone and oil to a dull surface. There is also the little-used oil finish which requires a prodigious amount of rubbing of linseed oil into the wood; this is particularly adapted to walnut.

It seems to us that varnishing is undesirable, and that as between wax and French polish, it is largely a matter of individual taste so far as looks are concerned, but that there are differences in desirability.

A very good choice of these finishes seems to be this: that for mahogany made before the close of the Chippendale period, wax is the preferable finish, but that from the beginning of inlay and veneer French polish is the better, because, except in the hands of some expert, and perhaps even then, the steady use of wax, with its attendant hard and rather rough rubbing, is too dangerous a process to be kept up year in and out on inlay and veneer. The oil finish should be completely barred from use on inlay and veneer on account of the action of oil on glue. French polish is peculiarly suited to work on inlay and veneer. It was first thought of for that use. It binds these applied surfaces of wood under a skin of hard and durable shellac-formed polish.

For oak of any period, wax is ideal; for solid mahogany it is good. For walnut, wax or linseed oil rubbed on by hand gives an admirable result.

An important matter of finish in chairs and sofas is that of the fabric used in covering them, and there are some very general rules as to bringing out the best effects in old chairs, as, if a chair-frame is entirely hidden under upholstering it can carry either the largest patterned chintz or the smallest according to the personal taste of the owner.

If there is pronounced outline in furniture—bold shape, and such curves and feet as those of an Empire sofa—a plain surface like velour gives the eye an opportunity to see the shape, which is not the case when there are floral effects in the upholstering.

Fine, graceful, delicate chairs, like Heppelwhite and Sheraton, show best in silk of fine geometric designs—in stripes, or in finely wrought small patterns—reproductions of the weaves of the early periods. Such a thing as a Gobelin pattern of wool tapestry on a Sheraton chair is an anachronism that hurts.

Chippendale suggested many things for his chairs; and who should know better than he what best suited them! He suggested that their seats be covered with the same material as the heavy window curtains of the rooms in which they were to stand, and he favoured dull red leather when they were to be used in a dining-room.

TWO EXCELLENT EXAMPLES OF SHERATON SIDEBOARD, GREATLY
ALIKE; BUT WITH ONE, THE TYPICAL REEDINGS RUN TO THE
TOP; WITH THE OTHER, ONLY THE LEGS ARE REEDED. THE ONE
WITHOUT THE LITTLE DRAWERS ON THE UPPER CORNERS IS THE
OLDER AND MORE DESIRABLE SPECIMEN.

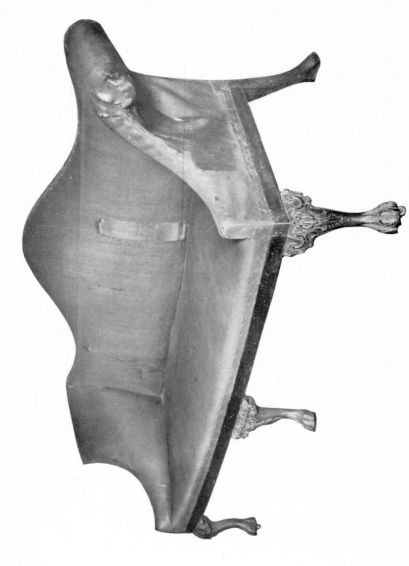

A KIND OF WRECK REMARKABLY WELL WORTH RESTORATION; A CHIPPENDALE OF REVOLUTIONARY DAYS.

Handles, on desks and highboys and chests of drawers, are an important feature in finishing and are not to be lightly chosen just because they are "quaint," although there are persons who actually select handles for their old furniture on no better basis.

Neither are handles necessarily right merely because they are found in place on an old specimen, for many an old piece has had its handles broken and then the entire frontage of handles has been replaced. We know of a Heppelwhite sideboard that within the memory of people now living has possessed three different sets of handles.

Old furniture must be given the right shapes and kinds of handles; the wrong handles injure very greatly the appearance of what they are on; and there are fortunately cabinet-makers' supply shops that furnish reproductions in old-looking finish. If your desk or highboy possesses its original handles its value is greatly increased. Next to that good fortune, it is occasionally possible to fill out your old set from some broken set.

Often the original handles left markings that are to some extent a guide in choosing the proper kind, but genuine old pieces equipped with original brasses, and contemporary pictures of such pieces, are the only safe and final guide. And one really needs to have not only the right design but the proper proportionate size.

In giving the charm of a fitting finish, there are thus found to be important the right kind of upholstering, the right kind of polishing, and the right kind of handles—as the wrong, with any of these, would give a handle to criticism!

CHAPTER XIX

THE CHARM OF THE UNEXPECTED

IT is really a pity that the good old word "Colonial" is falling into disuse as a descriptive term for old furniture. By the general usage of American collectors and lovers of the old it has come to mean not only furniture of literally the Colonial period but also such as was made during the years of Heppelwhite, Sheraton, of the early Empire—the long period of beauty: that *ancien régime,* in furniture, which has vanished quite away. But the general application of the word to years after we ceased to be colonies gave opportunity to dealers in antiques to apply it so much further as to make it include the highly undesirable designs of even as late as 1840 or 1850; thus increasing their sales by applying the attractive term to great quantities of the unattractive, the unbeautiful, even the positively ugly, which the uninformed or unwary would purchase under the magic of the old-time name. The word is still largely and properly used in its meaning of a few years ago; it is too fine, too excellent, and too American a word to be given up by those who know its proper application; but it has to quite an extent been spoiled for general use by the dealers' misuse and the hasty adoption of this misuse by many who should have known better. And there are some, both collectors and dealers, who, familiar with Jacobean, Chippendale, Adam, and so on, subtract the desirable known names from the sum of old-time furniture and call merely what is left "Colonial."

But the misuse of a name by dealers does not mean that all dealers are unreliable. There are, indeed, some who are altogether so; there are others who are reliable toward those whom they deem experts or even genuine lovers of the old; there are others who are practically reliable with all. There are antique shops where one should expect to find nothing that is honestly old, there are shops where the genuine and the imitation are intermingled, and there are shops where the truth is told.

For our own part, we prefer the leisurely collecting that permits of finding prizes in original sources and out-of-the-way corners, for each purchase thus becomes a triumph or at least a pleasure, and the pleasure continues throughout years. To buy altogether or even principally in shops is like shooting chickens in a barnyard as compared with the delights of hunting game in the forest. But there are dealers whom it is a pleasure to know, on account of their real love for their calling and for the curious and important finds that they from time to time make. Such dealers are usually in small country towns in regions rich in relics of the past—but also, it must be kept in mind, there are dealers in such places who pretend to be sincere gatherers of the old but who really receive their stock by carloads from central shipping points of imitations. There are also some excellent dealers in the large cities, although in many city shops, even where there are some genuine pieces, the genuine are almost lost amid a huddle of deceptive copies. Still, any collector would be very unwise to bar antique dealers altogether; it is possible that you may obtain from them just what you want and what you would never otherwise or elsewhere come across. They devote their entire time to the subject, whereas the amateur can give but a small part. And their charges for the right things must fairly include the price of their time.

The demand for antiques is increasing, while in the very nature of the case the supply must be gradually diminishing, and this gives strong temptation to make and sell the fraudulent—especially when so many people seem eager to be deceived. It is a case of "where ignorance is bliss." Many a dealer feels justified in selling an over-ornamented imitation as real because he knows it pleases many of his customers better than would the genuine.

But we have known of excellent finds in antique shops, both of the cities and of the smaller towns; and one find that was made by a friend of ours was certainly unexpected.

For he was on the way to his wedding, in the conscious grandeur of his wedding clothes. It was in Brooklyn. He was driving happily on, full of thoughts of wedding and bride, when his eyes fell upon a fine, a superfine, old dressing-glass and stand in an antique dealer's window! We shall not say that bride and wedding were forgotten, for they were not, but the true collector possesses a sort of sixth sense that tells him of antiques even when his mind is busy with something else. And the dressing-glass was so fine!—just the thing to secure on one's wedding day—just the thing for the bride to look at herself in!

The so-soon-to-be bridegroom glanced at his watch. There was barely time. Of course he could not be late for the wedding!—but the dressing-glass was tempting enough for the risk. So he stopped the carriage, skipped across the sidewalk and into the shop, hastily looked at the dressing-glass, saw it was good, bought it, hurried back into the carriage with it in his hands, unwrapped, for there was no time for paper and string, told the driver to hurry, and arrived, just in time, at the church, the proud possessor of a relic of the past!

He has since specialised largely in Hispano-Moorish pottery, finding his opportunity through official appointment abroad, but he declares that never has he felt keener delight and surprise than at that unexpected capture on his way to the church.

In collecting, the unexpected is always happening. In a sense, indeed, and a very broad sense, every find, in the very best kind of collecting, is unexpected, for the prizes come as the result of constant watching and constant seeking, with no warning of the moment at which a desk, a sideboard, a table, may be discovered. And yet, conversely, it may be said that even the most unexpected find is really expected, for one comes to take the surprising, the unusual, the astonishing, quite as a matter of course. It is almost impossible to surprise the seasoned and experienced collector. But although not really surprised, he is always pleased, for with every new acquisition, no matter how many things he has already found, there comes a new and keen delight.

A collecting friend, an architect, chanced to look down from his third-story window one day and there, on the crowded sidewalk below, was the unexpected sight of a man carrying a fine old wooden mantelpiece. It was not a moment for delay and at once he called down, taking the whole street perforce into his confidence: "I'll give you ten dollars for that mantel." "Sorry, suh," came up the reply. "I'se just got fifteen!"—and although that particular effort was a failure, the incident pointed out anew that at any moment Opportunity may be seen.

An ardent collector of old china, an English actor, played three seasons ago, in London, in a scene where he entered carrying a bowl, which by reason of apparent sudden fright he each time dropped and broke. The play had been running for a long season and he had broken over a hundred bowls.

Then, one night as he started on for the scene with a bowl which the property man had just handed him, he saw that it was a choice old punch bowl of Liverpool-ware with a fine black ship in the bottom. He could not bear to break it—he had barely a moment to spare —he dashed for the property man, who had bought ten second-hand bowls for the part that very morning from a barrow-vendor—in an instant he clutched a common one and dashed back just in time to break it at the proper instant. And how he does treasure that queerly-found punch bowl! He calls it his "Luck of Eden Hall."

The theatre, however, is responsible for a large number of antiques that are not antiques, and this has come about most curiously. For many a play has been staged in one of the periods of fine furniture, with much of the furniture made especially for the play, but not always for much more than looking at; and in the course of time, when the play was quite over its vogue, and no other play could use its pieces, they would be set adrift among second-hand shops; and this accounts for many a hybrid and apparently quite unexplainable specimen, not precisely right, yet not altogether wrong!—chairs, sedan-chairs, Venetian chests, tables. We know of a strange set of supposed Dutch chairs, bought by an acquaintance at a shop near the Great White Way—

chairs of pine, not well enough made to be excellent as
impostures, but just well enough to show as real things
at the distance of the stage.

The possibilities of the unexpected are endless. A
good old hand-woven blue and white coverlet was discovered on an ironing board and rescued before it was
scorched; an admirable brass candlestick was secured
from a Virginia pickle barrel where it had been placed
for the delightful purpose of making the pickles a
brighter green; an old coloured woman told us one day
that she had an "antee" we might like, and we did, for
it was an excellent copper-lustre jug; and the way in
which an Italian jar, of dull yellow, came to us was surprising. We had seen just such an old jar in Naples,
of precisely the desired ancient lines, but it was rather
too much marred, and besides there would be trouble
in carrying it, so we were to pick one up in Palermo,
our sailing port. But in all Palermo there was none to
be found, and keenly did we regret the unacquired
Neapolitan. Our steamer was reached by rowboat, for
it was anchored half a mile or so from shore, and it was
loaded light and stood high above the water, and the
deck was climbed to by a series of outside stairways, up
from a landing stage. From the deck we looked down,
over the rail, at the busy scene far below—and there, in
a little boat, was just the jar we wanted! A man and
a boy were in the boat, and a basket of lemons, and this
jar full of water, and they were making and selling

lemonade to whomsoever, about the lower part of the ship, they could attract. It was a time for instant action, and so the series of ladders was rapidly descended and the boatman signalled. He rowed close while the boy, by primitive and easy method, made ready some lemonade. "I should like to buy that jar"—For a moment the man did not comprehend; then a look of determination came into his face, for it was clearly an opportunity not to be missed, this of selling to a foreigner. "Three *lire!*" he demanded, firmly—only sixty cents!—And then he solemnly emptied the jar into the bay; he handed it over; and he and the boy rowed back to shore, their day's work happily concluded—while the yellow jar remained ours; a jar old in itself, long used, and very, very old as a survival of precisely similar jars made for many centuries. It is of common earthenware, but its colouring, of yellow in soft blending shades, and its shape, give it real distinction; and associated with it is the sense of delightful adventure and achievement and unexpectedness.

But one need not think it necessary to go far from home to meet with the unexpected. An acquaintance of ours, in Georgia, a State not as yet so searched over as is most of the East and South, is fortunate in that she lives in a part of her State that was missed by Sherman's army. She began, not long ago, to collect the old, and has already been surprisingly successful although her searchings have been restricted to her home town and to little towns near by. A few months ago she wrote that she had actually found a sideboard. It was of rosewood, and from her description was of the style of about 1860. Ought she to buy it? But there is really no 1860 furniture worth owning. And in spite of the attractive name, rosewood has not been used for the most excellent furniture. The sideboard was clearly one of those undesirables, hulking and heavy, that the beginner must learn to avoid. It would cost, to restore and polish, quite as much as one of beauty—and once invested in would remain a possession. So our acquaintance did not buy.

But this very morning—and we say this to show that it is at any time, at the present time, to-day, to-morrow, that chances come and that the discoveries were not all made years ago—this very morning, another letter came from our Georgia collector, and she has found her sideboard—although not quite sure of it! She sends a pen-and-ink drawing, showing it to be an adorable Heppelwhite. But she hesitates: "It's all of satinwood, and I don't know that I should like a large article of furniture all of satinwood." All of satinwood! The opportunity of a lifetime! So characteristic of its designer's best ideas; so few of them made in such fine wood; so few to find. The sideboard, it seems, belongs to an old lady to whom it has come down from a great-grandmother. "Do you think I should make a mistake to get this?" And our friend adds, in tribute to its gentle, graceful beauty: "The proportions of an old sideboard seem so much better than new ones."

We were motoring one day, some distance outside of the city of Philadelphia, and passed an open field where stands a granite stone bearing the inscription that at that place Fitch invented the steamboat; and the date given is previous to that of Fulton. Philadelphia does so dislike to acknowledge New York priority or superiority! That there is neither pond nor stream nor house near by and that there never was a pond or stream near by, strikes one as odd in view of the nature of the claim; one cannot help regretting the reticence of the marker, who refrained from giving the full explanation. However, it was an unexpected and interesting thing to come upon—but in a few moments we were to come upon something still more interesting; at least to ourselves.

It had begun to rain, and rain hard, and the top of the car was up, but none the less we noticed that we were approaching a rather attractive dormer-roofed house, of whitewashed stone, with a pretty door, prettily fanlighted. The house was rather gaunt, as if it had seen better days, and the surroundings were on the edge of bareness. The house was sheltered by three or four tall white pines, rising sheer to a hundred feet or so and not till then sending out their branches. Very dignified and very sombre did these guardian trees appear, and they were quite as old as the old stone house.

THE ADAM CHAIR, OF GEN-
EROUS PROPORTIONS AND
HIGHLY   ATTRACTIVE
SHAPE.

THE BIG FIRESIDE CHAIR
FROM MARYLAND.

LOOKING INTO THE SUNKEN GARDEN.

We were going rather fast, in that nervous haste that comes when the rain is trying to blow in upon you—but not too fast to catch sight of an Adam chair, right out in the rain, beside one of the trees.

The car was backed up and stopped, and in the rain the chair was inspected. It was even better than it had seemed from the car to be. It was an armchair, extremely comfortable, of generous proportions and highly attractive shape, and with the structural feature, characteristic of this type of chair, of being made in a straight line from the bottom of each front leg right up to where the arm curves toward the back. The chair was of ash, with framework so sound and firm that it felt, on shaking it, as tough and firm as a hickory stick —but the seat had gone!

A man came out, in the rain, seeing that a stranger was there. No, he said, the chair was not cared for by anybody. And for fifty cents it was purchased and taken in triumph to the car and somehow stowed in and carried home.

The lack of a seat was only a temporary drawback; it had originally been of rush, and merely needed taking to a rush-seat maker to be rehabilitated.

That is something, of course, to consider—that many of the prizes that collectors secure, for small sums, need to have something done to them before they are usable. Therefore, in strictness, the total sum expended should be considered as the price. In the case of this chair, there was the personal trouble of getting it home, and of taking off a coat of kitchen-coloured red paint and repainting; and there was the cost of the rush bottom, which was two dollars and a half—a quite customary price nowadays, in the vicinity of the large cities of the East.

And rush-seating is a most interesting kind of work. Just tip up a rush-seat chair and look at the underside; note the intricate difficulties of twisting, weaving and building—much more difficult, with a chair like this, which is broader at the front than the back, than as if the seat were precisely square. Come to an understanding of the skill and patience of this old-fashioned kind of work and you will never regret the expenditure necessary for it.

Adding the seat price to the original cost makes a total of three dollars—one never counts the home paint pots—but what a chair for three dollars! And it should not be overlooked that, so far from the absence of a seat being a drawback or a disadvantage, it was really the old chair's very best point—for if it had not been seatless it would not have been sold to us for fifty cents, would not have been out in the rain, would not have been discovered, would not have been sold at all!

As it is, at what a cheap price has romance been secured—for it is veritable romance to go swiftly along a public road, discover a fine antique, get personal possession of it and with it go on your way. It is like the old-time knight-errantry; the going about, along the country roads, in search of adventure, and rescuing the afflicted and distressed; and surely this fine chair was both afflicted and distressed!—and just as surely it was rescued.

At this moment, we have no doubt that there are hundreds of good old chairs and settees, standing neglected on porches or set outside of doors, ready to be saved, and meanwhile becoming daily more dilapidated. Many of such discards have been painted green; really, it may be set down as an axiom, that everything painted green should be heedfully looked at. Green paint is a great disguiser.

Only a couple of weeks ago a friend dropped in for a friendly call, and after a while remarked that on a road a little out from Valley Forge, at a blacksmith shop, where he had that day stopped for some minor repair work, the blacksmith was using, as a resting place for chisels and hammers, a little Empire table with two drawers! Although not a collector, our friend has at least an interest in antiques and really knows a good deal about them; and so we believe that the little table is really a good Empire worktable, and we cheerfully pass the suggestion along for it may be quite a while before we go over that distant road ourselves and meanwhile the table, unless rescued, may at any time go the final way of all flesh—or at least of all neglected old tables.

Oftentimes one comes unexpectedly upon some fine old mansion, or some village of large and comfortable houses, tucked away at quite a distance from any main-travelled road, and in such places there is often something desirable to be found from the very fact of isolation; and one wonders how such fine, big houses came to be built so isolatedly, and then realises that in early days, before macadam roads and railroads, one road was as good as another and offered just as good advantages for living and business.

We know very well a wife who collects and a husband who doesn't and as they were motoring through the country the wife saw the tall posts of a four-poster used as corners in a chicken yard and implored her husband to stop, but he only poked the chauffeur and said: "Put on speed, Mrs. J—— is seeing things!" And she has never found the same road again!

A man whom we know, from time to time makes hurried business journeys into the South, and he always looks particularly from the car window in passing through Princess Anne, in Maryland, for he knows that anything is possible at a place so delightfully named! And each time he sees, evidently neglected, an unusually fine Windsor chair, a tall comb-back, at a neglected door. Three times has he seen it, three times he has resolved that next time he must arrange to stop off and get that chair, three times his business haste has made it impossible. But another time!——

Yet the beginner must not make the mistake of thinking that everything left out of doors is discarded, for many a collector carefully keeps his prized and painted porch pieces properly upon his porch. Some of Washington's Windsors were kept on his terrace at Mount Vernon, for use and ornament—but not for sale!

We know a lady who socially made a pariah of herself in her summer neighbourhood, by speeding up the front steps of prosperous houses and trying to buy every old chair she saw advantageously and pridefully set out for summer use!

The unexpected may be anything. It may be little or big. A kinsman—this was some years ago—secured in Edinburgh a door from the chapel in the house of Mary of Guise, mother of Mary Stuart, a door with exquisite Renaissance carving. The old house was being torn down to extend a street, the West Bow, and he knew of the carving and happened to be there and found that the door was purchasable and purchased it and built it into an old part of his own home. At the old rag fair at the Marché du Temple, in Paris, we secured, for almost nothing, some undoubtedly genuine Sèvres. Somehow, nothing seems absolutely impossible of attainment when one realises that the splendid and costly furniture and fittings of the Tuileries were open to any Parisian to go in and help himself. It was such things as that which made possible the magnificent Wallace collection now in London.

A huge old Portuguese bottle, of three-gallon capacity, and of swelling rotundity as to form, caught sight of in a railway station and gladly exchanged by the agent for a modern demijohn to hold the family vinegar; a brass kettle and a candlestick picked up in a Western Reserve town, while waiting for a suburban trolley; the treasure being in a pile of scrap, mostly of brass lamps, that a junk dealer was actually hammering flat, piece by piece, to pack close for shipping; a big fireside chair, needing only upholstering, picked up in an old Maryland house for two dollars; a table offered by a man who said his wife wanted to have it chopped and burned to get it out of the way; a set of old diamond-paned windows, precisely what we wanted in altering our house, found thrown away in a corner of a barn loft; such are among our actual chance finds which point to myriad unexpected possibilities.

The village undertaker is likely to be a man who possesses old furniture or knows where it may be obtained, he being on hand when families are broken up; and from an undertaker of the Eastern Shore we bought a fine old bandy-leg claw-and-ball table. Boarding houses in the older portions of New York, Boston, Philadelphia, give excellent possibilities, for much of their furnishings has been bought piecemeal from other households or at local auctions. Real-estate dealers are likely to have a fund of curious old-furniture information. The quest is alluring and promising; the prize may at any moment be in your grasp. Kettles in junk, sideboards on flying trips, bureaus at auction sales, chairs almost anywhere.

CHAPTER XX

THE CHARM OF POSSESSION

THAT you have gathered antiques because they are intrinsically worth the gathering, that you have put them into your home as its furnishings, that there is nothing else with which you could so excellently furnish—this it is which makes the charm of possession, this it is which makes the chief and final charm of the antique. The things that you honour now were always worthy of honour; you would not willingly let them be lost; you are happy to be their possessor, for they are possessions of permanent pride.

Whether they have cost much money or little money is not in the least a matter of moment, for if they have been chosen according to the best standards they have the saving grace of distinction, and if they are veritable they have the mellowing charm of age.

We remember a description, by a cultured Englishman who visited the United States in the early days of our national existence and was entertained by Washington and other distinguished folk, of the home of the Binghams, who stood, socially, among the very highest of the time. And he describes their furniture as superb, and itemizes such things as the drawing-room chairs,

A ROOM TO SHOW THE CORRELATION OF OLD-TIME ACCOMPANIMENTS, SUCH AS FIREPLACE AND COR-
NICE, WITH OLD-TIME FURNISHINGS.

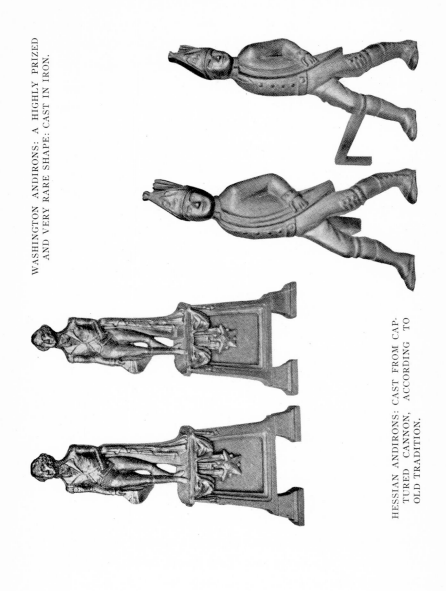

WASHINGTON ANDIRONS: A HIGHLY PRIZED
AND VERY RARE SHAPE: CAST IN IRON.

HESSIAN ANDIRONS: CAST FROM CAP-
TURED CANNON, ACCORDING TO
OLD TRADITION.

which were from London, "of the newest taste," with backs in the form of a lyre—evidently Heppelwhites. And that illustrates precisely what we mean—that the collector of to-day aims at obtaining the fine things of an era of fine things. "These were honoured in their generations, and were the glory of their times"; and they have the additional glory of a fine old age.

And possession does not mean that the quest of the old is concluded. One is always coming upon something else and either finding a place for it or taking out an article of minor importance and replacing it with the better one just obtained. And so the joy of acquisition, which was the beginning of it all, goes on, continuously, with the joy of possession, which is the end and aim of it all. But if possession were really a bar to further acquisition many a collector would imitate the New York man who not long ago disposed of all that he had gathered in order that he might have the joy of beginning all over again!

That the collecting of the rare and beautiful furniture of the past is not exclusively a privilege of the rich, cannot too strongly be repeated and emphasised. There are many things that only the wealthy can possess, but such things are not the final test of taste. It is shape, proportion, line, colour, that make one's furnishings good or bad, and these qualities may be possessed either excellently or poorly as the result of choice rather than expenditure. The collector need only feel sure that the prime secret of his home furnishing—and we are speaking only of that highest form of collecting which is for the furnishing of the home—is that everything shall at least be excellent and if possible beyond criticism; that he shall acquire nothing which is undesirable, objectionable, wrong. With this, his things may be and properly should be as fine as he can find. He should be content with nothing but what is good, and should hope and endeavour to have at least some of his things of the best. "A thing of beauty is a joy forever; its loveliness increases"—these, the most famous lines of Keats, admirably express the joy of the collector, for when he obtains a perfect thing of its kind his pride and his joy in the possession go on increasingly.

Simplicity is the keynote of all success in furnishing, and precisely the same with antiques as it is with things that are modern; and this brings to mind an acquaintance who had his home outfitted with fine "period furnishings," by a professional decorator. When the drawing-room was supposedly finished, the decorator gave it a long and final survey, with its admirable cornice, its white-pillared fireplace (with the mantel empty except for two candelabra standing in front of a long, low mirror), its chairs and tables, its rugs, its hangings of ribbed velvet reaching to the broad white window-sills. He walked about. He altered the positions of the chairs to a greater informality. He looked carefully over every detail. "There is something else needed," he said quietly; and the owner was quite prepared to hear him order some ormolu, some piece of glorious Sèvres; something, in short, that would be costly, and would come from his own establishment. "There is something else needed—ah, now I see!—you should get half a dozen geraniums, in their plain red flower-pots, and put them on the white window-sills, for the touch of greenery and colour and the homelike effect." And such simplicity is illustrative of what is at the very heart of all effectiveness.

The collector who possesses to hoard has always existed and will always exist. "What toil did honest Curio take, what strict inquiries did he make"—thus sang Matt Prior many a generation ago, for collecting seems to be the satisfying of a natural instinct and has always had a vogue; and Prior goes on: " 'Tis found, and O his happy lot! 'Tis bought, locked up, and lies forgot." But the collector who collects for his home is not in the least of this kind. He gathers things to live with, to be part of his daily life, to touch and handle, to look at and to use; he takes honoured things of the past into his possession and they become honoured things of to-day. To gather, throughout years of pleasurable enjoyment, to search for antiques as fate and fancy lead, to "prove all things and hold fast that which is good"—that is the collecting which gives resultant charm.

In the face of all the stately and exquisite work that one's ancestors knew, it is curious to find that there are good Americans who look on the fine past period as one of mere primitiveness, and who actually believe that comfort and beauty came in with their childhood and the age of golden oak. But most Americans have learned the beauty of the furniture of the past, and freely offer the further tribute that should be given to things of fine and dignified age.

To many a beautiful thing of age there comes a patina, a faint and delicate incrustation that time alone can give; and there is also a figurative patina which, with the passing of years, gives to a thing of beauty a fine and incommunicable charm.

It is delightful to collect. It is delightful to acquire and to possess the beautiful and admirable things of the past. And the collector finds that the tender grace of a day that is dead is still, for him, delightfully alive.

INDEX

INDEX

303